BLOOD, OIL and SAND

BLOOD, OIL
AND SAND

RAY BROCK

THE WORLD PUBLISHING COMPANY

CLEVELAND AND NEW YORK

FIRST EDITION

Library of Congress Catalog Card Number: 52-5192

THIS BOOK IS FOR MANDY

ACKNOWLEDGMENTS

The author thanks The Washington Post, The Montreal Star, The New Orleans Times-Picayune and States, The Memphis Commercial Appeal, The Dallas Morning News, The Kansas City Star, The St. Louis Post-Dispatch, The Denver Post, The Worcester Telegram and Gazette; the Turkish newspapers Vatan, Cumhuriyet and La Republique, as well as The American Broadcasting Company, for invaluable background material originally incorporated in news dispatches and broadcasts sent from the Middle East and now indissolubly coordinated in the over-all story of Blood, Oil and Sand. Sincerest thanks to Marguerite Bloch for her careful editorial assistance.

RAY BROCK
Istanbul, Turkey

BLOOD, OIL and SAND

1

LIKE A WAYWARD HURRICANE, the tricky and devious storm center of the East-West struggle for power is moving slowly but inexorably into the low-pressure area of the strategic and immensely oil-rich Middle East. In all the two-million-square-mile land mass of Middle East, encompassing the vital waterways, the oil sea that lies beneath the baking deserts, the pipelines, refineries and dock areas, the emotional and political barometers are set for storm.

From the fortress of Gibraltar to the Afghan frontier, Soviet Russia and the increasingly dangerously divided Anglo-American governments, peoples and oil interests are interlocking in deadly conflict that can lead only to a third World War, or almost unthinkable compromise. Unthinkable because the pattern of Soviet power and conquest is based, thus far unalterably, upon the eventual penetration, subjugation and exploitation of the peoples and the riches of the mighty Middle East—and because British and United States policies are linked, however unwillingly, for Middle Eastern defense at all costs, including war.

Appalling as these conclusions may seem, they are based upon the cold, considered opinions of the European, American and Middle Eastern governmental and military authorities entrusted with the destinies of the Middle East, its fabulous riches and its volatile Islamic peoples. Intrigue, propaganda, political murder, smuggled arms and endless funds are only the lightest weapons at Russia's disposal. Communist agents have been infiltrating the Arab world since well before the end of World War II and, fanning the flames of Arab nationalism and religious fanaticism, have whipped up a growing holocaust which may only too soon engulf this oil-laden area.

Laggard and misdirected Western diplomacy, coupled with the "Sahib mentality" of old, British Middle Eastern hands —and the abounding greed and selfishness of the oil-wealthy and cotton-rich Iranian and Egyptian satrapy—serve only to add fuel to the bonfire.

The stakes in Middle East are enormous, and nobody knows this better than the Russians. Desperately oil-hungry and vulnerable at Batum and Baku to aerial or land assault, and virtually encircled by a thin but narrowing perimeter of Western air and naval bases, Russia's strategists can see only too plainly that their timetable for Middle Eastern conquest rapidly is being disrupted. Russia's Korean adventure and the probings in Indo-China were linked with assassinations, cabinet upsets and prolonged crises in Iran, Hashemite Jordan, Syria and the Lebanon, Iraq and Egypt, in a campaign to keep the West off balance and gain time for Russian complots elsewhere in the Middle East and the Balkans.

The expanding violence of the emergencies in the Middle

[4]

East has forced a commensurate expansion of the territories lumped together in the sandy wastes, the towering mountains, swamps and tidelands and the filthy, disease-ridden villages and cities extending from Morocco to Afghanistan and beyond. The term "Middle East," which years ago began to supplant the more familiar "Near East," is justified by the continuing exigencies of defensive coalitions aimed now at blocking Islamic nationalism and swift penetration by Russia from the north. The term itself is British, military, for-the-use-of, and presently encompasses all the predominantly Islamic countries including Morocco, Algeria, Tunisia and Tripolitania, Libya, Egypt, Jordan, Jewish Israel, the Arabic Lebanon and Syria, Iraq, Saudi Arabia and the Yemen, Aden, Oman, Kuweit, Bahrein, Iran, Afghanistan, and, more recently, Pakistan. While Turkey looks Westward, the Turks are an integral part of Middle Eastern Defense, as are the Greeks, and World War II proved that Yugoslavia could not be excluded from the order of battle in the holding action in Crete and the dogged denial to the *Afrikakorps* of precious supplies bound through the Balkans to Cyrenaica.

A handful of archaeological purists and cartographers may quarrel with this arbitrary enlargement of "Middle East." Their quarrel, however, lies with current history and the juggernaut of power politics, and the cold logic of strategic air power, armored divisions and logistics to supply armed forces across thousands of square miles.

Any attempted analysis of Middle Eastern civilization, as it bears upon the deadly crises menacing this vital area and the rest of the world, would be bootless and herculean midway in the twentieth century. Anthropology is fascinating—and embroidered history doubly so—but it will be the task of *Blood,*

[5]

Oil and Sand ruthlessly to eschew encyclopedic flights and romantic legend and stick to the clothesline of hard fact.

It was engrossing in mid-June of last summer to clamber down into the massive diggings of the University of Pennsylvania's archaeological crew at Yassi Huyuk, the probable site of ancient Gordion, in the blazing Anatolian desert sixty miles west of Ankara. A hundred and twenty-five sweating Turkish diggers were unearthing, seventy-five feet down, bits of bone, bronze and pottery to prove that here, indeed, had existed a civilization extending back to perhaps 2300 B.C. Around the rims of the three major craters on the dig were scattered the "finds," the bits and pieces of urns, perfume bottles, arrowheads, rusted amulets and rings attesting the culture of the ancient peoples who had dwelt in splendor on the once-rich plateau. And here, too, lay proof that Alexander the Great bivouacked his legions along the Sakariya River in 333 B.C. This was a rich oasis, even after the downfall of successive civilizations, on the spur route connecting the ancient camel caravanserai spanning the Asiatic wastes to "The Golden Road to Samarkand." About two thousand yards southwestward of the dig, however, on the heights dominating the deep, yellow-muddy, swift-running Sakariya, I paced off the winding ruins of the Turkish trenches—site of the bloody Sakariya battleground, high-water mark of the Greek campaign against the Turks in 1923.

Even as I studied the terrain below through binoculars the shimmering, heated air stirred strangely, and then came the distant crumping of shellfire from the mountains toward nearby Polatli. Two Turkish batteries were hurling 105-millimeter howitzer salvos into the hills. A pair of observation planes circled lazily over the target area. Then there was the distant whistle of one of the new American locomotives and a long, slow freight wound its way through the valley below, bound eastward and upward toward Ankara. Through the binoculars the train's cargo was plainly visible—tanks and jeeps and hooded howitzers, a pair of bulldozers, then more tanks and more artillery. Attached to the rear of the freight were four of the familiar, rickety, wooden third-class carriages used by the Turks as troop transport. The carriages were bedecked with star-and-crescent banners and Turkish soldiers were hanging out the compartment windows. These troops were a part of the fresh contingents bound for south Turkish seaports and trans-shipment to Korea.

Back at the dig, there was fresh excitement. One crew had unearthed, in a corner of the second excavation, a great urn which seemed to be almost intact. Dr. Rodney Young, the University of Pennsylvania's archaeological expert, personally was supervising the delicate work of extracting the new "find." Dr. Young's four aides, three women and a young man with a dusty crew-cut, hovered anxiously over the urn, scraping nervously now and then at the exposed area of the treasure and admonishing the Turkish diggers to take great care. The Turks shrugged and took it easy. Down here in the pit it was 125 degrees Fahrenheit for most of the twelve-hour day—with wages three liras per diem, or roughly one American dollar.

Tramping the blazing two miles back across the sandy wastes to Yassi Huyuk and the dig's hostel (our lone jeep had gone off to a nearby burial mound), I paused from time to time to listen to the rumble of the Turkish artillery, to watch a wedge of Turkish fighter planes roar low overhead bound for Etimesught airdrome, three bombers flying high and north-eastward and then the afternoon commercial flight from Istanbul to Ankara. Just past the *arroyo* below the squalid huts at the edge of the community, I came upon four workmen engaged in building a big new house. Like its neighbors, it was rising, tier on tier, with mud-brick, but this house had a wooden framework, genuine windows and boasted eight rooms. Clearly, this was to be a mansion. I halted awhile to watch the work. A small, barefoot boy brought water in a rusting oil-barrel drawn on a rickety wagon by a spavined, miserable horse. One of the workmen funneled the water into a wooden tank, then skillfully scooped the tank half full of dirt. His companion, meantime, was adding double handfuls of straw to the thick, muddy concoction. When it reached the proper consistency, the shoveler scooped the mixture into a crude, wooden mold which made six bricks at a time. His assistant then took the farther end of the mold and they lifted, together. Half a dozen big, thick wet bricks rested on the board beneath. As the brick-maker shoveled in his next batch of mud, he called to one of the workmen working with a trowel on the upper story.

"Hayde!" he snapped. The man upstairs laid by his trowel, shouldered a hod and walked down the steep, swaying homemade ladder from the upper story. He loaded his hod by hand and, leaning forward, shouldered the hod and walked back up the ladder with all the grace of a mountain goat. No hands.

"Cok guzel!" I said, the Turkish equivalent of a bravo. The hod carrier paused on the last rung of the rude ladder, executed a kind of *do-si-do* by stepping rapidly three steps downward and upward again, to land on the platform. He grinned down. The shoveler and his assistant had stopped to watch the byplay. They grinned, too. The waterboy was back, also grinning. I squatted in the narrow shade beside the corner of the new house and opened a pack of cigarettes, extending them to the workmen. Work stopped immediately. The hod carrier and his fellow bricklayer came down the ladder two

[8]

steps at a time. We lighted cigarettes, squatting in a row in the shade, and made desultory conversation. Desultory Turkish was about my limit, after seven years' absence.

Mustering his courage, the shoveler, pulling at an imaginary goatee and grinning, pointed with a forefinger to my dusty beard and said: *"Ticani?"* This was a fine joke, fairly standard, but a joke, nonetheless. The Ticani, pronounced *tee-jahn-ee*, are a Moslem religious sect whose members wear beards as a mark of their faith.

"Hayir—yok, effendim!" I laughed. *"Amerikan, gazeteci!"* This was also a joke. With Bob Stevens, a photographer, I had been in the little community of Yassi Huyuk overnight, quite enough time for the news to spread for miles around that American journalists had descended on this archaeological outpost in the Anatolian wilds.

Would we take pictures and write about the folk dancing tonight in the square below the hostel? I said we certainly would.

We had come to Yassi Huyuk from Ankara, the capital? How? By train, I explained, to Polatli and by U. S. Army jeep from the artillery school.

Ah! and did we not think that the Turks were *buyuk askari?* Great soldiers? We certainly did think so.

Formidable gunners? And had we seen the Turkish *askari* use the bayonet? Indeed, we had.

Then the sixty-four-dollar question: *"Harp geliorum?"* Is war coming? Five earnest, bronzed faces stared at me fixedly. *"Effendim?"* pressed the shoveler. I nodded slowly. Sooner or later, I said, maybe sooner than later.

There was a moment's silence and then everybody talked at once. The shoveler, Hassan, had lost his brother in Korea. Another brother had volunteered and was taking his final training at Ankara before embarkation for the Korean fighting. Hassan, himself, would volunteer for Korean service after the July wheat harvest. The young hod carrier was tapped for his military service in September. The grizzled bricklayer silently opened his dirty, sweat-stained shirt and bared his chest. A pale, ugly, jagged scar extended from his right collarbone down to his belly. A Greek had done this thing, he explained, right here at the battle of Sakariya, with a bayonet. The Greek, he added, was dead. The small waterboy was clamoring to be heard.

"*Kore gitti! Kore gitti!*" he piped. All of ten years old, he was announcing his enlistment for Korea.

Passing around more cigarettes, I saw the mud in the trough drying and hardening in the late afternoon sun. Hassan caught my eye and shrugged. "*Maleesh,*" he said, "so what?"

Walking on to the hostel some twenty minutes later, I found Hassan's assistant, the straw-mixer, following me at a few paces. He tagged along doggedly with that shambling peasant gait that eats up the miles, but he said nothing. Just outside the compound near the hostel I stopped and turned to him. He stopped and stood staring at the hard-baked earth.

"*Effendim,*" he said gently. There were tears in his eyes. Slowly, he rolled up the filthy cuff and the long sleeve that all but covered his left hand and his arm. The arm was withered and the gnarled hand hung at the end of it like a claw. "*I would have made a very good askar,*" he said. He stiffened and his right arm snapped up in a salute that would have done credit to a Scot's Guard. Wheeling abruptly, he strode back down the sandy road as if he were marching to music.

2

EMBATTLED TURKEY is at once a semi-isolated defensive bastion, the Allied right flank and the heartland of the Middle East. The Anatolian Turk, from the lowliest peasant to the most cultured and traveled Ankaran, is a fiercely nationalistic, proud and individualistic human being. The new Turkish army and the Turkish nation were constructed upon the flinty bedrock of this character. It is a character at once primordial—as exemplified in the savagery of the Turks in mortal combat—and as adroitly tricky and devious as the best brains the West and Russia have been able to muster through two centuries. The rough, tough, hard-riding plainsmen who stormed down from the Asiatic steppes between the seventh and tenth centuries to overwhelm the Arabic and Persian tribes of the grasslands sired the Seljuk Turks, the ancestors of the rugged peoples who are today the allies of the West in modern Turkey.

Warriors and poets, artisans and tradesmen, peasants and

bankers, twentieth-century Turks are a distillate of the Anatolian Turkish conqueror Osman of the fifteenth century, Genghis Khan and the mighty Mustapha Kemal Ataturk who alternately led and bulldozed his peoples from the corruption of defeat to the heights of victory.

It is from those heights and the mountain defiles and passes of the rugged Taurus mountains and the defenses-in-depth of wild Anatolia that Turkey's full-strength twenty-seven divisions looked down this past winter and early spring upon Russia's mounting forces in the Caucasus and the nearby Balkans. While the Western powers feverishly juggled arms allotments and monies for the Middle Eastern defenses, the Turkish government and General Staff coolly appraised enemy maneuvers and made slight alterations in the Turkish order of battle. As Whitehall and Washington reshuffled their diplomatic staffs throughout the entire Middle East, the Turks gravely greeted new envoys, apprised them of the shifting sands and stormy waters of policy on Turkey's six frontiers and bade them welcome.

At Paris, Rome, London and Washington, meanwhile, and in countless unpublicized and even unsuspected conferences in Middle Eastern capitals, Turkey's superb corps of foreign envoys continued to hammer home the self-evident truths of the spreading crises in Middle East, seeking formulas, compromise; extending *aides-mémoires* coupled with grim warnings that 1952 was very probably the year of ultimate decision, war or peace, between Russia and the West. In almost every instance, the Turkish communications have stressed that when war comes, if it does come, the primary battleground will be the Middle East. The realistic Turks have sought to drive home to the inflamed Iranian regimes and to Iraq, Syria and the Lebanon, Hashemite Jordan and the unhappy, dragon-driven Egyptian leaders that unplanned, bootless revolution is madness.

With almost monotonous and pitiful regularity, Islamic leaders from all the Middle East have trooped through the Turkish capital at Ankara. Bereft of ideas and allies, openly afraid and nearing moral and spiritual as well as actual bankruptcy, Syrian and Egyptian emissaries, Iranian special envoys, Jordanian plenipotentiaries and minor sheikhs from the lower Persian Gulf have beseeched Turkish support against the nationalistic Frankenstein monster fashioned by the corrupt governmental satrapy which until recently kept burgeoning desires for liberty and decency of living in a percussion-cap box. To all such entreaties the Turks have turned a ready but reasoning ear.

Iran was counseled more than a year ago, in Ankara, to a policy of moderation in the nationalization of the Anglo-Iranian Oil Company. The Turkish Foreign Office informed the Iranian Ambassador, Mohammed Said—a moderate who knew it anyway—that the British had been pushed as far as they would go; that the Mossadegh policy of "kick the British out" was virtual national suicide, and that the Communist Tudeh party would overwhelm any Iranian administration which pursued the tactic of strangling Iranian economy by shutting down the oil wells and stoppering the Abadan refinery. Mohammed Said, a longtime friend of the writer, dutifully relayed the Turkish counselings and is in national disgrace in consequence. The Tudeh party has made greater inroads than in the 1943–46 period when it almost swung the phantasmagoria of an "Azerbaijani Republic" in northwestern Iran.

Egypt followed suit. The plight of Egypt is directly traceable, as the Turks tried to explain, to a colossal blunder on the part of the erratic Wafdist party, which controls former Egyptian Premier Nahas Pasha, the then Foreign Minister Selah ed-Din Pasha, and the more moderate President of the Egyptian Senate, Zaki Ali Oraby Pasha. Because the wavering, dying British Socialist government had begun to expire on its do-nothing policy in Iran, the Egyptian regime was inspired to resurrect the hobgoblin of British control of the Suez Canal and the presence of British troops in the Sudan. Recognizing the gravity of this situation, the Turks struggled to arrest the heavy-handed Egyptians during the opportune meeting of the Inter-Parliamentary Conference at Istanbul last August—totally unreported in the American press—but too late.

Zaki Ali Oraby Pasha stressed to this writer in Istanbul and later on shipboard that the Egyptian rioting was merely a manifestation of suppressed nationalism; that reason would prevail, and that Farouk, who was still gambling along the Riviera at the time, would return to Egypt to bring order out of the beginnings of chaos.

In Turkey, however, as early as mid-July there was no such sanguine belief. The Turkish Foreign Office kept its sensitive fingers upon the Middle Eastern pulse and forecast with deadly accuracy the steady deterioration of Anglo-Egyptian relations through the late summer and early autumn of 1951. The extraordinary Turkish Intelligence Service, which had warned of a complot against King Abdullah of Hashemite Jordan, murdered a scant few weeks later in Jerusalem following his Ankara visit, forecast the assassination of Riad el-Solh of Lebanon, and warned of another *attentat* against Colonel Adib Shishakly, behind-the-scenes ruler of Syria.

It all came true. Furthermore, Turkish warnings of trickery in Iran, Egypt and Pakistan, and the murder of Liaquat Ali Khan, evolved as predicted.

[14]

Turkish foreign policy in the dangerous summer of 1952 is aimed, as always, at the absolute preservation of Turkish territorial integrity and the maintenance, if possible, of peace in the Middle East. Peace—but not at any price. Having lived cheek by jowl with the treacherous Russians for centuries, and having fought them every forty years during the last two hundred, the Turks have no illusions about their neighbors on the north and east.

"Russia will attack," Turkey's Foreign Minister told me in Ankara, "when the Russians are convinced the Western powers are sufficiently mutually suspicious and divided. The Middle East is virtually helpless. Turkey alone can and will defend itself, with the aid of the United States and Britain and the North Atlantic Treaty Organization Powers, we hope. In any case Turkey will fight. We do not fear Russia. We fear no one. If it has taken Korea to prove the mettle of the individual Turkish *askar* (soldier), well and good. As we interpret your American phrase, we knew it all the time."

These forthright views of the Turkish Foreign Office were echoed by Turkey's extraordinary envoy to the U.N.—Selim Sarper, a fifty-year-old rock-hard career diplomat and ten-year friend of the writer.

"Had NATO admitted Turkey and Greece to the North Atlantic Treaty Organization one year ago," said Sarper, "the entire Middle East crisis might have been averted. Egypt, one year ago, would have fairly jumped at the chance to join Turkey and other Mid-East states for mutual defense.

"Moreover," continued Sarper, "Iran would have modified its demands upon the British, and the British themselves would have been more reasonable."

Selim Sarper is a powerfully built, disconcertingly severe-looking Turk with what can only be defined as an arrogant

[15]

nose, a mobile mouth and a gentle, persuasive voice which can ring out suddenly with the peremptory command of a Prussian officer. Short of severe illness or an unlikely bullet, Sarper is an inevitable candidate for Turkey's Foreign Minister portfolio, ultimate premiership and possible presidency. He is an accomplished judo expert, a boxer, a fine swordsman and a crack pistol shot—all useful attributes in the murderous Middle East. Almost single-handedly Sarper drove through the U.N. Political Committee the condemnation of Red China's invasion of Korea and the attack upon U.N. troops. Heading the *ad hoc* Committee on Greece at Paris, Sarper demonstrated immense diplomatic finesse in piloting his committee between the Scylla of outraged Greek nationalism on the one side and a bizarre coalition of Arab and South American states and the delighted Russians on the other—a more dangerous Charybdis. Sarper is a man who enjoys the confidence of virtually every delegate to the United Nations, save the Russians and their satellites, and he commands their unlimited respect.

These, then, are the Turks. The writer feels an almost irresistible compulsion to enlarge upon personalities, living or dead, to point up the Turkish *mores,* the fibre of the people, to consider the great ones, including the incredible Ataturk. *Blood, Oil and Sand* is concerned, however, with the present and the immediate darkling future.

Traveling in the uplands of Anatolia, by liaison planes, jeeps, horseback and afoot, I had a perhaps unrivaled opportunity to assay what the Turks themselves think of their future. Nearly four years of association with the Turks in World War II provided bona fides enough. If I wanted to see a "classified" airdrome I saw it. The new jet strips were my oyster. Gun emplacements, new tanks and bazookas, "secret" maneuvers and specialized tactics fresh from Fort Knox, Bragg and Quantico figuratively were laid in my lap. Toward the end of June 1951, I was privileged to witness, with the cream of JAMMAT (the Joint Allied Military Mission to aid Turkey), one of the most impressive war games I have ever seen, including war itself.

It was a three-hour-and-forty-minute exercise, involving a reinforced infantry regiment supported by two tank companies, two batteries of howitzers (light) and four batteries (heavy). The "shoot" was staged at Ayash, some sixty miles west-south-west of Ankara in a gigantic Napoleonic valley. The targets and objectives were three graduated ridges (Able, Baker, and Charlie, of course) commanding the vast plain below our vantage some 800 feet above. The "shoot" opened precisely at 3:45 with a deafening series of rounds of TOT (Time on Target) in which Turkish gunners zeroed-in light and heavy howitzer shells, followed by mortar fire. The artillery worked over Able ridge until it was obscured by a dust cloud so dense as to preclude visibility. Then from three miles away the infantry came on at a dead run, in heat of 150 degrees Fahrenheit, flopped, laid in mortar and machine-gun fire, and advanced again.

Precisely on time, again, four Turkish light bombers, then four more, roared in over the neighboring mountains and laid phosphorus, HE and napalm bombs squarely on Baker ridge. That was to nullify covering fire from the enemy. The infantry moved up, not jogging, but on a dead run. According to the exercise, then, the forward elements of the infantry had been pinned down by fire from Baker ridge. The tanks moved up, screened by Able ridge and smoke shells laid down from the rear batteries. Turkish engineers moved out behind the smoke screen, vetted a simulated mine field and waved on the infantry and the tanks. Up came the infantry on the double, with bayonets now, and mounted Able ridge as fresh as daisies. The tanks ground on ahead, blasting the rim of Baker ridge with deadly cannon and machine-gun fire. The howitzers and mortars were moving on across the ridge to plaster Charlie.

This was war. Through the gathering haze over the vast baking valley, one could spot the support troops moving up at a steady run. Now they sprawled and in a matter of moments were firing their mortars and heavy machine guns over the heads of their advanced unit at Baker ridge. Three miles away, down the valley, one could spot the third infantry wave coming on, bayonets fixed, running like the wind.

Charlie ridge blew up. Every battery had let go with TOT. The valley shook and reverberated and rocks and loose earth plummeted down from our cliff-side eyrie. Then the tanks moved in, spitting red fire and dotting Charlie ridge with devastating accuracy. The infantry, incredibly, went scrambling up the ridge at a run.

Suddenly it was over. The tanks wheeled and lumbered off in perfect formation toward the rear. The infantry companies scrambled down the hill and fell in. The air, thick with dust and cordite fumes, hung motionless under the broiling sun.

"Juda-a-as Priest!" I looked over my shoulder. It was General William H. Arnold, Chief of JAMMAT and no tyro. Veteran of Guadalcanal, conqueror of 10,000 Japanese on Cebu, the general was wiping his sweaty brow and still studying the terrain below. "Some show," he muttered. He turned to me. "Did you see *that?*" he demanded rhetorically. "Five miles on the double and up those ridges?" The general was definitely an infantryman. I nodded. "Judas Priest!" he repeated. Down below, the jeeps and staff cars and limousines were hooting and honking, and now one of the general's aides was plucking at his sleeve.

"General Arnold, sir," he was saying, "there's the buffet with the General Staff, sir, and you are due at JAMMAT before the Ambassador's, sir, and—"

The general shook him off and took one final look across Ayash valley, still swathed in the dirty, shimmering dust, with the Turkish troops moving out below. The heavy smell of cordite was almost overpowering now in the blistering sun.

"Every tank, every gun, every shell, every bomb—American," said the general. "And every man on the trigger a Turk. And they said we couldn't do it." The staff car was hooting again and the general turned away, with a nod. I slid down the hill through the thick dust and sand and back to my jeep, thinking:

These, then, are the Turks . . .

3

Stepping off the Ankara *Ekspresi* from Istanbul onto the gray concrete pavement of the Turkish capital's sleek, modern railroad station, the casual traveler gets the impression of barren, antiseptic, almost Teutonic cleanliness. If he stays close by his hotel and away from the cellars of the Ankara Palas, dines, as most foreigners do, at old Baba Karpich's fabulous restaurant, and limits his strollings to the broad boulevards and parklands, he most likely will retain this impression. But let him wander out the back streets and into the old city or up the hills to the *Kale*, the fortress, and the unmistakable effluvia of the Middle East smites his nostrils as sharply as in Baghdad, Alexandria or Cairo—a weird and in time fascinating odor compounded of soft coal smoke and spices, urine and open-work sewers, garlic, onions and the stale sweat of unwashed bodies and garments, mud and ancient moldering rock, cheap perfume, fresh fruit, the casual manure of horses, goats and children, the fetid, lingering stench of old amours.

Ankara and Turkey reek with old amours, real and fancied, romantic as a slave boy scaling a wall to the inner sanctum of an ancient *hareem* or professionally contrived as an Armenian flesh merchant bargaining with a wealthy stranger for the favors of a belly-dancer in some noisome *boîte* in Galata. Ankara and Istanbul are very nearly all that Eric Ambler and Oppenheim have written in their somewhat lurid but excellent novels, with splendid local color and fine ears and noses for the sounds and smells of the Turkish capital and the fabulous old city on the Bosporus. The simple fact is that espionage, sabotage, narcotics, cheap murder and the highly profitable sale of women are pursuits which do not flourish as abundantly or publicly as these prolific English writers would seem to imply.

They do flourish, however. Not even the Turkish secret police have been able to eradicate the corruption of centuries in old Constantinople, and Ataturk's dream of Ankara as a pure, incorruptible capital went glimmering with the feverish days and gaudy nights of World War II when illimitable wealth was poured into Turkey from a score of foreign capitals to seduce and traduce enemies on neutral ground. It is no exaggeration to disclose that Turkey today harbors, albeit distastefully, as complicated a series of systematic, deadly espionage rings, saboteurs, drug merchants, jewel and gold smugglers, killers-for-hire and lovely, available women as ever existed in wartime Lisbon, Switzerland, Stockholm or Turkey itself through the period of 1939–45.

It was for many of the foregoing reasons, and for many others, that I established headquarters in Ankara to cover the seething Middle East during the summer and early autumn of 1951. Viewed narrowly from the earthworm vantage of the archaeologist or historically from the bookworm site of the anthropologist, the Middle East would seem to fan out in comfortable, orderly concentric circles from somewhere midway along the eastern Mediterranean littoral, much in the manner of Mr. R. M. Chapin, Jr.'s, authoritative maps in *Time*. In actuality and from a newspaperman's point of view, however, the suppressed storm center of the entire Middle East lies in Turkey. The answer is quite simple. Much of it is imbedded in the opening chapters.

Turkey is a listening post nonpareil upon the entire Middle East, the adjacent Balkans, Central Europe and Soviet Russia. There is not one nation in the entire Middle East, with the possible exception of Saudi Arabia, which could not be overthrown overnight by a well-planned, organized and swiftly executed *putsch* or *coup d'état*—except Turkey. No other Middle Eastern state is so chock-a-block with prime diplomats who receive, automatically, copies of every foreign-office dispatch in transit between the Middle Eastern capitals and Moscow, Paris, London and Washington. The Turkish Foreign Office frequently is hours, days and even weeks ahead of rival governments upon burning issues affecting not only the Middle East but Korea, Germany, the Baltic, and internal affairs as reflected from Washington, London, Paris and Moscow.

No other nation is allied so meaningfully to the West as Turkey. The presence in Turkey of the most powerful, efficient and highly operative military mission ever dispatched abroad by the United States was and is a guarantee that American security is linked inextricably with Turkey's. While General Eisenhower stormed, pleaded and almost begged for armed support from Western European powers, and a stepped-up arms program in the United States, Turkey stood resolutely with twenty-seven armed, trained and highly maneuverable divisions in northeastern Anatolia and in Turkish Thrace.

Moreover, I was among friends. Real friends are hard to come by in peace or war, but I had somehow penetrated the recesses of Turkish reserve and suspicion during nearly four years of correspondence from Turkey during World War II. This was a new government, it is true, the "demokrasi" of President Celal Bayar and his Democratic Party which almost miraculously had overthrown the semi-dictatorship of Ismet Inonu and the Ataturk Old Guard in May 1950. Bayar's government is a still imperfect democracy in the Western sense, shot through with fumbling, fearful bureaucratic blunders, but a government of determined Turks, nonetheless.

Turkey is still a backward, Westward-looking nation of some 21,000,000 rugged peoples, with a constitutional government, woman suffrage and compulsory schooling, and an embattled army of nearly 400,000 enlisted men and 22,000 topnotch officers. Within a fortnight Turkey could put nearly 2,000,000 men in the field, and ultimately could muster nearly 4,000,000 fighting men, some of the best in the world.

Weighing the Middle Eastern balances, I found the scales tipped heavily toward the Turks. Here was transport to all quarters of the Middle East. Here were communications. Here lay the front lines of any war to come. The Turks faced the Russians, as they have done for centuries, on the Caucasus, across the stormy Black Sea, and now from Bulgaria in the Balkans. More important, here were news sources, background material and *a people you could put your faith in.*

Beyond Turkey's eastern frontiers, the Anglo-Iranian oil war was under way. The major news services and the handful of independent newspapers which still employ foreign correspondents sent their writers into the battle of the communiqués. The battle raged for months on end. A comparative analysis of AP, UP, INS and Reuters' dispatches, plus the

[23]

"specials" of the *New York Times,* the *New York Herald Tribune,* the *London Daily Express,* the French and Swiss correspondents and the "stringers" of various Middle Eastern journals, readily discloses that the 200-odd newsmen who rushed into Iran might have saved themselves the time and their auditors the money. A pooled dispatch twice a day would have covered the communiqués issued by Mossadegh, Mossadegh's emissaries to the Abadan refinery, the official spokesmen for the Anglo-Iranian Oil Company and the strangely jarring pronunciamentos of the U. S. Ambassador, Dr. Henry F. Grady, and the British envoy, Sir Francis Shepherd.

A much more serious, more sedulous and deep-laid story was developing on the Middle Eastern front—and the date line was Ankara.

King Abdullah of Hashemite Jordan had petitioned the Turks for permission for a royal visit. Abdurrahman Azzam Pasha, the winning, genial Secretary General of the Arab League, was to follow Abdullah to Ankara. Riad el-Solh, Lebanon's gangsterish but warm-hearted strong man, was to follow him. Then in succession were to come the Arabic leaders of Egypt, the Persian Gulf sheikhdoms—Kuweit, Qatar, Oman, Hadramaut—and perhaps Colonel Adib Shishakly, the kingmaker of Syria. Iraq would send Nuri as-Said, and Ibn Saud of Saudi Arabia would dispatch one of his elder thirty-five sons to wrap up an Islamic-Arabic alliance in the Middle East.

It was a pretty picture from the Arab point of view. Abdullah had the limited blessings of Attlee's Socialist government. Abdurrahman always had a claque in London, due to his Oxonian accent, his sweet reasonableness vis-à-vis the thorny problem of Palestine (in London), and his extraordinary double talk in the Middle East. Riad el-Solh had the

Lebanon in his pocket, including the notorious Beirut "water-front gang"—and the Arab longshoremen *ran* Beirut, or so the story goes. The Trucial sheikhs were fat and happy: Anglo-Iranian and Aramco (the Arabian-American Oil Company) already were promising fabulous cuts on oil royalties. The sheikh in Kuweit, Mosullah Bey, has been collecting $164,000 daily since August. Ibn Saud had just signed a fifty-fifty royalty deal with Aramco. *He* was happy. Said Pasha of Iraq was making noises like boosted royalties on Kirkuk and Mosul, but Abdullah had told him firmly, "Shush!"

There were only two unforeseeable errors. One, the Turks gave King Abdullah a festive but noncommittal welcome. This could be glossed over, and was. The Arab press, led by the round-the-clock Arab News Agency, pointed out that Turkey's President Celal Bayar had given King Abdullah of Hashemite Jordan an extraordinary reception at which the Turkish Prime Minister Adnan Menderes and Foreign Minister Fuat Koprulu had engaged in deep, studied converse with the king. Afterwards, he chatted privately with President Bayar. Having had a private quarter-hour audience that afternoon with Abdullah, and a later hour-long briefing at the Turkish Foreign Office, I could not believe that Abdullah had got what he came for, namely, Turkish backing and the Turkish aegis over a new Islamic alliance in the Middle East. (A private conference with Abdurrahman Azzam Pasha confirmed Abdullah's failure.)

The second unforeseeable error was Abdullah's insistence some six weeks later upon attending the shrine of the Mosque of the Rock in Jerusalem. As he stepped out of his sandals and prepared to enter the Mosque, a tailor's apprentice named Moustafa Shukri Aysho stepped quickly from behind a pillar and shot him five times in the face and chest. Abdullah fell dead. His assassin shot himself before he was riddled by Abdullah's bodyguard. The killer's record was clear. He had been hired by henchmen of the Haj Amin el Husseini, the former Grand Mufti of Jerusalem, who took a dim view of Abdullah's efforts to unite Araby against Communism, splinter revolt among dissident Egyptians and Jordanians and the miserable Palestinian DP's, of whom Aysho was a member.

The story goes deeper than this. Moustafa Aysho was a "terrorist," the term for any Middle Easterner today who uses firearms or high explosives. He hated Israel. He had been carefully taught. Abdullah was a symbol of hatred to young Moustafa, who, incidentally, had been promised rescue by the Mufti's bully boys. Had he survived Abdullah's slaying, he almost surely would have been murdered by the Mufti's cohorts. The Mufti and the Communists prey upon susceptible, fanatical Arab youths in the broiling bazaars of the Middle East. Abdullah himself lived a rough and murderous life and killed his enemies like flies. So, as a matter of fact, did the Seljuk Turks.

As the world knows, Riad el-Solh of Lebanon was assassinated four days later. Nobody is quite sure whether he was killed by his own erstwhile henchmen, rooked by the subtle connivings of the clever, hard-boiled Lebanese gangster, or by the Moslem Brotherhood, who were determined to spike his projected junket to Turkey. At any rate, Abdullah's dream of uniting Araby, like his dream of a "Greater Syria," went glimmering. Abdullah's maniacally Anglophobe son came out of a Swiss rest home to bestride the Hashemite throne, and as Tallal the First he remains there today, insolent, arrogant, viciously opposed to any Western influence in the Middle East. Tallal apparently is politically blind to the Russian encroachments from the north, in which he would be the first victim.

The Turks had given me the word, weeks ahead. Turkey was having no part of the murderous intrigue of their Middle Eastern neighbors. Nor are they having any part of Arab terrorism today.

Turkey, itself, has been euchred into a fronting position for the Arab League by the sheer power of Turkey's present position among the dissolute, divided Arab states. Turkey faces west, with her glistening bayonets pointed eastward. The Turks, among all peoples in the Middle East, recognize responsibility.

The night soil of Turkey may smell the same, and the Turks on the lower levels may go in rags and with vermin, but there is an indomitable spirit abroad today in modern Turkey. It will not be denied.

4

THE FIRES OF IRAN cast an ominous glow across the length and breadth of the mighty Middle East. Flickering, flaring, dwindling only to burst forth again, the crises in Teheran and Abadan afflict the Arab states like the undulant fever which haunts the pestholes around the Mediterranean littoral. The mock-sinister arsonist in Iran's yearlong conflagration was balding, spindly neurotic Dr. Mohammed Mossadegh, who alternately screamed, wept and fainted his way to power over the Iranian Majlis—the lower house of the emotional Iranian Parliament—and plunged his country into the throes of bloody revolution.

"Man is not the creature of circumstances," however, according to the quill of Benjamin Disraeli. "Circumstances are the creatures of men." At any rate, the assassin's bullets which felled Premier General Ali Razmara of Iran simultaneously unleashed precisely the proper climate for the theatrical buffoonery of Mossadegh and his bodyguard and heir apparent,

Hussein Makki. While the outlawed Communist Tudeh party sent its "spontaneous" demonstrators howling and screaming through the streets of the capital, Mossadegh used the off-stage noises to the maximum advantage. So did the Communist agents who had infiltrated Iranian Azerbaijan and its capital Tabriz, in the northwest; Kazvin and Teheran, ninety miles eastward. Speaking to the surcharged Parliament, Mossadegh had to pitch his voice even higher than usual in order to be heard above the chanting, yelling street mobs which filled the spring night with battle cries of *Death to the British! Iran for Iranians! Nationalize Our Oil!* and *Kill the Infidels!*

Mossadegh finished his peroration with a hymn of hate for Britain, the British and the Anglo-Iranian Oil Company, demanded the "nationalization" of the billion-dollar oilfields and the Abadan refinery—and fainted. The thud was heard 'round the Middle East; even as the Majlis voted to oust the British and take over Anglo-Iranian, all manner of hell was breaking loose throughout Iran, in nervy Iraq, Syria and the Lebanon, Hashemite Jordan and Egypt.

In his Egyptian sanctuary in Cairo, the swart, bearded Haj Amin el Husseini, ex-Grand Mufti of Jerusalem, summoned his henchmen for a conference on strategy. The hour was ripening for this murderous little man to unleash, with all the unlimited guile, gold and guns at his disposal, a vast wave of shootings, stabbings, bombings aimed at inciting forty million Arabs throughout Islam to a *jehad*—a Holy War—against the despised infidels.

While the British and American diplomatic missions at Teheran with almost consummate ineptitude fumbled away their eleventh-hour chance of a *rapprochement*, Mossadegh and the Mufti entered into an unwitting alliance with Com-

[29]

munist operatives bent upon driving Western interests and Western ideals forever from the bloody, oily sand of the Middle East.

In Iran, the "mad" Mullah, Kashanix, signaled his National Moslem Holy Warriors that the hour had struck. Teheran radio carried inflammatory orations to the peasantry and the tribesmen, the Lurs, the Bakhtiari and the Kashgais, and to the heretofore tractable, well-paid Iranian workers in the rich oilfields at Masjid-i-Suleiman, Maidan-i-Naftun, White Oil Springs, Haft Kel, Agha Jari and the vast subsidiary fields which dot the plains of southwestern Iran below the towering Zagros mountains. Iranian workmen listened with disbelief to the repeated, semi-hysterical announcements from Teheran radio that Iran, at long last, was "free."

The pumps kept working. For the long weeks through the almost intolerable heat of the Iranian summer, the rich fields continued to pour their precious yield of high-grade, paraffin-base crude oil in unending streams through the interlocking maze of pipelines to steaming Abadan and its mighty refinery on the broad Shatt-al-Arab river. The end, however, was coming. Mossadegh had miscalculated, disastrously. Either that—and one can start a fight quicker in Middle East with this argument today than debating the beard of the Prophet—or the fanatical Iranian leader had failed to calculate at all. In the light of later events, this latter presumption is highly questionable. At any rate, the outraged British abandoned the fruitless diplomatic talks at Teheran and cracked down with characteristic British efficiency.

From Aldershot in England, the British rushed their Sixteenth Independent Paratroop Brigade, 3,000-strong, to Nicosia, Cyprus, just four hours' flight from Abadan. A massive fleet of British "Dakotas"—DC-3's—began ferrying the wives and children of British oil engineers from Abadan to Cyprus and on to England. The engineers followed. Tankers from the fleet of the Anglo-Iranian Oil Company—the world's largest— lifted their hooks and sailed out of the harbors of Khorram- shahr, away from Abadan and away from the dangerous, muddy and pestilential anchorages off the noisome mud-flats of Bandar M'Shur and Bandar Shahpur. The empty tankers, riding high in the dirty-yellow, crocodile-infested waters of the Shatt-al-Arab, were replaced by a bristling British cruiser, three sloops and a gunboat.

Throughout the Arab world, meantime, the press and radio were screaming *Gunboat Diplomacy!* In late summer this was still grist to the mill of Mohammed Mossadegh, Hussein Makki, Mullah Kashanix and, elsewhere in the embroiling Middle East, to agents of the murderous Moslem Brotherhood and to Communist agents who were inciting street demon- strations and riots under the banners of *Arab Nationalism* and *Death to Imperialism!* Moscow stepped up its Arabic language broadcasts to six and finally to twelve per day, blanketing the bazaars and oases over millions of square miles with pre- fabricated horror stories of Anglo-American atrocities in the Middle East. Atrocities there were none, as later shamefacedly attested by Arab authorities.

Abdullah's slaying in Jerusalem and Riad el-Solh's murder within the week touched off new violence in a dozen quarters. Moscow radio, caught in its own absurd trap—Arabic lan- guage broadcasts had at first attributed both assassinations to "Anglo-American gangsters"—abandoned this theme and charged the killings to "gallant Arab nationalists."

It was the *Ramazan* religious holiday, notoriously the most dangerous period in all Islam. Mohammedans fast from sunup to sundown, and with the boom of the *Ramazan* cannon they tear into food and drink like peoples possessed. Already drunk on the heady wine of what to many a Moslem seemed genuine Islamic revolt against the West, with fiery *arak,* or *raki* from the bazaars in his belly, many a tough Arab went berserk. It was touch and go for three uneasy weeks among the dwindling British colony now huddled in the awful heat of Abadan, and distinctly unpleasant after dark for all Westerners in isolated areas of the Middle East.

Flying back to Turkey from a sudden junket to the British paratroop base at Nicosia, I found that the fanatical *Ticani* had burst into violence. Some 300,000 strong in Turkey, these bearded Moslem buckos had stormed into Ankara, Istanbul, Tokat and Corum to smash busts and monuments of Ataturk. *Ticani* violence is directed primarily against the memory of Mustapha Kemal Ataturk because the great Turkish leader ruthlessly suppressed the Mohammedan faith wherever he found it impeding Turkish progress. The *Ticani* violence in Turkey, however, was minor and short-lived. The tough Turkish police jailed the ringleader, rounded up some four hundred of his cohorts, and the show was over.

Circumspectly, however, the Turkish Sûreté redoubled the personal bodyguard of President Celal Bayar. Somewhat annoyed by these precautions, the Turkish President took a leaf from the book of the late Ataturk and former President Ismet Inonu and stalked unceremoniously into the gardens of Karpich's restaurant, accompanied by no one save his personal aide, Colonel Yaver. The titillated public, Turkish and foreign, was totally unaware of the six husky well-armed Sûreté operatives who sat just inside the restaurant and waited uneasily for the Turkish chief of state to finish a defiant, leisurely dinner. The maître d'hôtel, Edvard, signaled me when the president had been served his coffee. Walking across to Bayar's

[32]

table, I distinctly heard the *snick* of a cocked revolver, but I kept walking. The Turkish chief of state was hospitable and obviously relished the opportunity to put his security cordon in its place. He dwelt at length on the Turkish Army war maneuvers at Ayash, ducked a direct question on Turkey's views vis-à-vis the North Atlantic Treaty Organization and parried a query about the *Ticani* demonstrations. Afterward, I had a double brandy at the bar. A burly Turk in a dark blue, double-breasted suit appeared at my elbow. I recognized him. He was a member of the president's bodyguard.

"You really ought to be more careful, my friend," he murmured in French. "I know you and four of my colleagues know you. But the fifth—*Tiens!* He is a new man. He thought you were *Ticani!*" He turned away. I told Nazim to give me another double brandy.

Back at the hotel, the sleepy hall porter handed me a message from my tipster on the Istanbul newspaper, *Vatan.* Richard Stokes, the hard-boiled field chief of the Anglo-Iranian Oil Company, had been prevailed upon to make one more effort to come to terms with the Iranian Government. And radioed Washington dispatches reported that the White House had delegated W. Averell Harriman as an unsolicited mediator in the continuing crisis over Iranian oil. I wired KLM at Istanbul for reservations on the Wednesday plane.

Iran is an old line of country to any correspondent who has covered the Middle East as anything but a visiting fireman or a trained seal. With Hank Gorrell and Hal Peters of the *United Press,* Cedric Salter of the *London Daily Mail* and a dozen other correspondents, I had learned it the hard way in the 1941 invasion. Flying down to Cairo from Ankara on an inside tip from the British, I joined eight other war correspondents in a four A.M. takeoff aboard a lumbering British

Imperial Airways airliner which set us down at Basrah, on the Shatt-al-Arab river. British and Russian forces already had begun the joint invasion, from the south and from the Russian Caucasus. We caught the night train to Baghdad, chartered cars the following morning and drove as fast as our steaming, boiling and outrageously expensive Chevrolets, Opels and Buicks could carry us, on the trail of the Warwickshire Yeomanry commanded by General William Slim, the Chief, now, ten years later, of the British Imperial General Staff. The 1941 trip was a wild, hell-for-leather adventure attuned to the mixed political cacophony of those days—Germany had invaded Russia a scant seven weeks earlier—and our major aim, after writing the popgun invasion story, was to examine the Red Army at first hand.

Flying out to Iran in 1943, I was again on a *New York Times* assignment, this time to write a series of dispatches disclosing for the first time the enormous role that the hitherto top-secret Persian Gulf Command was to play and was, indeed, already playing in the most ambitious logistics venture in world history. Joel Sayre later put this story in his engrossing book, *Persian Gulf Command,* and this writer unreservedly recommends it as the truest account of the incredible job performed by Americans on the supply route to Soviet Russia. But that was another time and in fact another country.

Iran at the half turn of the twentieth century is indeed a vastly different country. Topographically it is the same, aside from the time erosion of ten years. Ethnically it has gone through no fundamental changes. The hordes of refugees, Poles, Balts, deserting Russians and Ukrainians, who fled to Iranian sanctuary during the war years have drained off into Turkey, Israel and overseas to America. Buttressed by the towering peaks and defensible passes of the Elburz range in the north and the Zagros, which extends from the Turko-Russian frontier in the northwest to the Persian Gulf and the Pakistan and Afghan frontiers, Iran should be one of the most impregnable plateau fortresses in the world.

It is, instead, one of the weakest, most corrupt, diseased and miserable nations on the face of the earth. Beneath the blood-stained sands of the Iranian kingdom lie the richest oil seas in the world, and on the surface dwell some 17,000,000 people of whom 95 per cent live on the level of animals. Two million are nomads, wandering with their starveling sheep and spavined horses in a near-hopeless search for grasslands.

Man-killing heat withers the high plains, and man and beast alike, in summer. Northern Iran in winter is attacked by a cold which I can only compare with the bone-chilling iciness of Madrid—"the little wind of the Guadarramas which will not blow out a candle but which will take a man's life . . ." Water is more precious than the national currency, which is now handed about in bales, like the drachmae of Greece. Congenital syphilis and gonorrhea, and a weird combination of the two which baffled American Army medicos in a freak outbreak at Hamadan in 1943, bestride all Iran, with tuberculosis, trachoma and glaucoma, typhoid, smallpox, typhus (in winter), malignant ringworm (which attacks and withers the scalps of Iran's children) and treacherous blitz invasions of bubonic and pneumonic plague. Hygienic lessons, in driblets from the West, have proved futile. It is an oft-told tale, for it strikes the casual visitor most forcibly, but the spectacle of Teheran at "water time" is horrifying. At specified hours, water is released from central floodgates into the openwork sewers of the capital. It gushes through the open sewers, carrying with it the offal and sputum and refuse from the filthy, windy streets. The tradespeople and beggars gather at the

[35]

curbs to drink, perform their ablutions and relieve themselves, rinse out clothing and household utensils, whereafter they scoop up the water in all available pots and vessels for household use. Poetic Persia still believes that *water which passes over stones is purified*. Lice-ridden beggars haunt the back streets—the Iranian *gendarmerie* use batons to beat them off the broad boulevards and avenues—and expose their skeleton-like frames and suppurating sores as they moan for money or bread.

If there is compassion for the poor, the hungry and the diseased in Iran, this writer has not seen it, and it is not for want of looking. Frightful and documented accounts have come out of concentration camps about what sheer hunger can do to "normal, civilized" people. And Iran, ancient Persia, was a birthplace of civilization. Alexander the Great was Persia's first conqueror twenty-three centuries ago, and the tides of empire have swept the Persian high plains ever since.

Iran's tyrant today is *want*. As in Egypt, a cruel and supercilious, avaricious financial satrapy controls the reins of government. The young Shah, Mohammed Reza, has sought somewhat more than half-heartedly to rectify the sins of his father, the vicious and corrupt Reza Khan, who was flung out by the British in 1941. Young Mohammed, however, is hamstrung by his willful, headstrong, moneyed deputies, and haunted by a misspent youth in which his profligate father indulged his every whim in convertible Cadillacs and Packards, wines and liquors and aphrodisiacs, and the cream of Teheran's young womanhood. Perhaps more than is generally suspected, the young Shah is dominated by his ruthless, driving sister, Princess Ashraf, who controls a kind of palace guard which, in turn, exerts enervating pressure upon Mohammed himself.

The Shah of Iran is a prisoner of indecision. Some hint of his ultimate fate stems from reports that he has transferred large sums in gold and foreign securities to banks in Lausanne and Zurich. Mohammed Reza does not strike this writer as a fighter. Both Mossadegh and Mohammed Reza left Washington empty-handed, but Mossadegh last winter was still fighting his weird campaign, usually from his bed.

Iran itself is a prisoner of fanatical childish pride and stupid or willful inaction. Half a million American dollars have been sent to Iran for locust prevention, but there is strong reason to suspect that the bulk of this fund was dissipated in handouts to bogus survey groups which surveyed nothing, including locusts. The Export-Import Bank has deposited $25,000,000 to the Iranian account, but this loan has been vociferously opposed by Iranian politicians, xenophobic to the core, and venal. The graft, bribery and corruption in Iran are commonplaces, gossip in the bazaars, where even the most penurious citizens seem to take a bizarre, perverted pride in the flagrant dishonesty of their rulers.

To this writer, who has covered a number of foreign and domestic newsfronts, the Iranian picture is dreadfully similar to that of Louisiana in the dying heyday of Huey Long. Blasted, blackened and condemned by documented records which proved his enormous malfeasance in office, his padded highway and building contracts, his downright crookedness, the "Kingfish" took to the Senate floor and screamed himself purple in the face to damn his accusers.

I was in the lobby of the Washington-Youree Hotel in Shreveport, Louisiana.

A snaggle-toothed, begallused oldster turned away from the scratchy radio newscast which had just relayed the Washington tidings.

[37]

"Well, suh," he said—*ptooie!* and the spittoon rang—"ol' Huey certny gave 'em hell today, didden he?"

The Iranian, or Persian tongue, is certainly little more polished, in the vernacular, than the rhetoric of Louisiana. Mossadegh was admonished to "Go to hell!" in the Majlis as recently as December.

"Plus ça change. . . ?"

5

War with Russia is the ineluctable fate of the West, now that U. S. power and influence in the Middle East have been so seriously undermined. No reasonable man, in the opinion of this writer, can persist in begging this question, indulging in the hair-splitting, caviling equivocation which has marked the sorry record of the U. S. State Department in its last-minute febrile attempts to expunge the existentialist character of Dean Gooderham Acheson and his associates. The record of ruinous U. S. Asiatic policy is exceeded only by that of the selfsame burrowing fellow-travelers in the Department of State who undermined the last vestiges of U. S. power and influence in the Middle East and the Balkans in the 1942–46 years, and in varying degrees thenceforward.

Oil-wealthy Iran lies supine before the Soviet steam-roller. Nuri as-Said Pasha of Iraq is a straw man, an opportunist who consistently has played off the British against the Russians and his restive Arab subjects, since well before the end of World

War II. Dynamic Syria is a time bomb, and the death of Syria's strong-man, Colonel Adib Shishakly, could spring the trigger. Shishakly, the target of no less than three *attentats* in the past year, is himself philosophic about it.

"If I die, I die," he shrugged. "If they get me, they get me. Maybe I take some of them with me—" and the Colonel flipped the screw on his holster and came up with a Luger. Shishakly is a crack revolver shot, an accomplished swordsman and, they say in the bazaars, a murderous man with a knife. Any and all of which may account for his extraordinary longevity in Damascus and all Syria, where loners are dead men. Colonel Shishakly has his faithful.

The bordering Lebanon is a problem. Here are 1,300,000 highly restive Arabs, half of them Christian, with a minuscule army but a propensity for violence. The Lebanon—like Syria, Iraq, Hashemite Jordan, Saudi Arabia, the Yemen, Egypt—is a member of the dissonant but occasionally powerful Arab League. Lebanon has less than 5,000 equipped and trained troopers in its command, but the Lebanese are a hardy, canny, street-fighting people. Because Beirut is a lush fleshpot of the Middle East, luxury-loving Russians have gravitated here. The biweekly payoff to Soviet agents in the Middle East is reputedly second in Beirut only to the swarming operatives in Turkey. Russian agents are prone to "go soft" in luxurious Beirut, so the story goes, at the St. George, the Hotel Normandie and the lovely villas in the hills, and the turnover in MVD men is the largest in the Middle East.

Tallal the First rules Hashemite Jordan with a quixotic hand. Abdullah's erratic son succeeded his murdered father at a moment when the British would much have preferred the younger, softer son Naif. Naif prefers Cadillacs, hashish, hard money and women, most of which are readily available. Tallal is something of a fanatic and, despite—or perhaps because of—his Sandhurst training in England's West Point, is violently Anglophobe.

Tallal is forty-one, dark, brooding and obviously mentally unbalanced. He was recuperating in a rest home in Switzerland from a nervous breakdown when Abdullah was shot in Jerusalem. Tallal hates Glubb Pasha, the British Commandant of the 15,000-man Arab Legion, the toughest and best coordinated fighting force in Middle East after the Israeli Army. Tallal summoned Prince Regent Naif to Switzerland, browbeat him into submission and flew back to ascend the Hashemite Jordanian throne.

Ibn Saud and his three and one-half million subjects have continued to play it quiet. Saudi Arabia is doing well. King Ibn himself is seventy-two, half-blind and increasingly sedentary. Saud wants no part of the Arab intrigue and Communist inroads in the Middle East. Established Communist agents usually are shot out of hand or, in some cases, left to the tender mercies of the Arab women who take particular delight in using their long knives on the tenderer parts of the invaders. Ibn Saud draws roughly $100,000,000 annual royalties for oil concessions granted the Arabian-American Oil Company. Saudi Arabia, however, has become the particular target of Soviet intrigue and, oddly enough, the capital Riyadh, as recently as the turn of the year, approved visas for more than twenty-five Soviet commercial agents interested in Saudi Arabian oil and, possibly, Dhahran.

Dhahran is an American air base on the Persian Gulf, north of Bahrein, and headquarters of the Arabian-American Oil Company, Aramco. Dhahran boasts airstrips which will take and launch the biggest bombers on and off the U. S. drawing boards. It is at once an army outpost and headquarters for the engineers of Aramco who roam the Middle East in quest of oil. This endless quest could explain the Soviet's demonstrated interest, or it might be merely a screened Russian mission aimed at discovering whether we can indeed bomb east of the Urals to Siberia from the airstrips, the bomb and ammo dumps of strategic Dhahran. The answer is we can.

Soviet envoys are swarming across the crisis-ridden Middle East today in numbers that should dismay our security officers in Washington. Bogus commercial missions thrust Communist Czechs, Poles, Hungarians and Bulgarians across vital and strategic frontiers with every passing train and plane. With cameras, notebooks and ciphers, Russian agents are pinpointing Western engineering projects, landing strips, roadways, fuel dumps and ammo dumps, barracks, staging areas, flak batteries and communications, assembly points, repair depots, motor pools, radar and sonar operations, meteorological surveys and intelligence operations—to the T.

Egypt is a special case. Spurred on by the willful Iranians, the Egyptian governmental hierarchy twined vine leaves in their collective hair and haplessly went mad last autumn. Apparently, it mattered not a whit to Nahas Pasha and Selah ed-Din Pasha that theirs would be the first heads to roll in any genuine Communist uprising. *Blood* was the cry and sand the domain, and the faraway oil of Iran, Iraq and the Persian sheikhdoms the ultimate "nationalist" goal in this fantastic leave-taking of the political senses.

Could Egypt defend herself and the Suez Canal? Was it possible that the Sudanese themselves would prefer to maintain the status quo, rather than risk a blow-up in Middle East at this time, and all that it might entail? Was it not, after all, deducible that Premier Nahas Pasha of Egypt and Foreign

[42]

Minister Selah ed-Din Pasha had, in the midst of a wave of nationalism, overplayed their hands?

The questions were mine, directed at Zaki Ali Oraby Pasha, Wafdist Party member and President of the Egyptian Senate. The answers were weird, obviously spooked. The place was an isolated corner in the forward lounge of the S.S. *Excalibur,* bound between Alexandria and Naples.

Egypt *could* defend herself, he said, the Suez and the battle stations of the Egyptian Middle East. The Sudanese relished independence under the aegis of King Farouk of Egypt who was, a few weeks later, to identify himself as "King of Egypt and the Sudan," and both the Egyptians' Premier and the Foreign Minister had interpreted precisely the mood and thought of the Egyptian peoples.

The president of the Egyptian Senate then disclosed a deep-laid plan of the Egyptian Senate to involve the United States in the Anglo-Egyptian quarrel. The Egyptian Senate was to invite a mixed commission of American Senators and Congressmen to Egypt, expenses paid, to study the thorny problem of the 800,000 Arab Palestinian refugees, but actually to be confronted by the British-Egyptian conflict over control of the Suez Canal and the Sudan.

"Was this ethical?" was the question. No less so, was the answer, than President Truman's proposal that W. Averell Harriman be sent to Cairo to settle an issue that was old when the presidential envoy was in knee pants. Britain had stood athwart Egypt for almost a century. Since when could "an American upstart, the paid, self-publicized offspring of a tough American railroader," hope to park his Homburg in Cairo and settle a problem that had baffled the best brains in England and the Middle East for half a century? The Egyptians, like the British, were incensed.

[43]

So much for Harriman. He was already on his way home, empty-handed. The Harriman mission to Mossadegh in Iran was an ignominious failure. Washington's efforts to bolster it as a "limited success" were worse than ludicrous, and were stamped by the successive failures of Assistant Secretary of State George C. McGhee's efforts to elicit any degree of compromise from Mossadegh in bedside talks. McGhee had been doomed to failure from the outset of the Harriman mission. What Mossadegh wanted was loot, American dollars, blackmail, lest he swoon (conveniently) into subservience to the Communist Tudeh party and swift Russian penetration of Iran. The inside story is that Secretary Acheson said "Yes"— the hard-boiled undersecretariat, advised by the House, said firmly, "Hell, no!"

Acheson finally prevailed, and Mossadegh got the money with no strings attached. Here was a problem. The issue is blackmail, pure and simple.

The entire Middle East wants, lusts after, must have, money. Turkey is no exception. The Turks need cash to fight. My tipster on the Istanbul *Vatan* used to come to me. "Look," was the line, "your Congress has whittled away another two million dollars! No help for Turkey. What are we to do?"

"We're out here," I said, "because we have to be, not because we love the Turks, or because you love us. We're in this thing together. Get used to the idea! The jets, the fighters, the bombers, the tanks, the airstrips, the engineers and technicians, the master sergeants, the officers, the ordnance we're pouring into Turkey is mutual defense. Those tanks, lights and heavies, and the howitzers and the mortars, are as much for you as for me, as much for your people as mine."

This sank home. There was a long silence. Then—"We need money," on a rising, almost Calypso-like timbre.

"You and who else?" I said.

Back in my hotel room at the Park Palas, I really chewed on this one. With half the Middle East aflame, a reasonably intelligent, thinking Turk could obscure ideals for money, ignore the real problems of the neighboring countries and quarrel with me about Congressional apportionments to the Middle Eastern countries.

What was it? *Amour propre? National Pride?* War, as the Turks know better than any other peoples in the world, is a settled affair: and the Turks will fight, as savagely and ferociously as they have fought before, against the Russians. What, then?

Faith, maybe. Endurance, perhaps. They don't quite trust the Europeans and the Asiatics, and I cannot quite blame them. The Korean masquerade has had a lot to do with it. We chuck in a hundred thousand American lives—and then lie doggo.

You tolerate the Mufti and his fellow-murderers, and you accept the errant slings and specialized arrows of outrageous fortune, and suddenly you're in trouble.

You survey the Middle East, and with care. Here is a land you've loved with a special love. Here are a tempestuous, volatile, religious and even fanatical people who really don't give a damn about how their lives come out. They really don't. They say they do in their rather stylized prayers, but they don't, really. I think it probably boils down to the fact that they don't have much faith in their altogether miserable lives. Backbreaking work through a twelve-hour day and home to a stinking pallet on an earthen floor and the surcease of a woman, tired and wan, who can offer nothing but her tired loins in a kind of travesty on love.

War is a specialized kind of thing. You would be surprised

how often it would please the missus. And the kids. At first. Anything for a change. The smell of cordite supplants the stench from the alley where the goats, the cattle and the children leave their manure. There is the bright, hot excitement of action, something different, something new. The kids squat around amid the crashing of the bombs, and they don't give a hang. They haven't the faintest idea what it's all about and they're happy. It's just noise.

Only they're children. What the war is about they don't know.

War *is* a specialized kind of thing, and it is horrible. Children, like bemused governments, wander into it. It is not pretty. Arms and legs and heads get blown off, and arms and legs and human plumbing are exposed, and untidy entrails and brains you would never see outside a hospital, if you're lucky, and that's war.

War is what we are heading into, straight as a die, and one can take his reading from the foregoing.

6

WE WERE FLUMMOXED again. Our angry little indigna-
tion meeting split up and a dozen hot, sweating,
war correspondents bore down, converging on the briefing
officer. One of us muttered something about "bloody old
Muddle East . . ."

"Don't use that term in *here!*" snapped Colonel Ivor Jehu.
"I'll have you know this is the *Indian* Army!"

It was, too. The place was Baghdad and the time a decade
ago but, aside from the cast of characters, it could have been
six months or six weeks ago, or yesterday or the day after
tomorrow. Around the frontiers of Iran and smoldering Egypt
and elsewhere across the bloody sands between the eastern
Mediterranean littoral and Pakistan, the British are sinking
deeper and deeper into trouble, but somehow muddling
through.

Or are they? The Baghdad muddle ten years ago was just
one more conflict of commands, contradictory orders and mis-

laid papers of accreditation for a dozen impatient war correspondents jumping off on the Iranian invasion, but it was
symptomatic of the confusion prevailing in the middle eche-
lons of the jealous Middle East Command and the proud
British Indian Army.

For an up-to-date reading on the muddled Middle East,
simply exchange the now-defunct role of the British Indian
Army for the American military missions swarming into the
Middle East, and as for the Middle East Command of the
British, well, it has not changed remarkably. The confusions,
the jealousies, remain and have multiplied.

Not much had been written or stated publicly about the
burning issue of the Supreme Command in the Middle East
before Churchill's visit to Washington in January 1952. It had
been too hot a potato even for Churchill himself, although he
had been needled into a couple of caustic remarks on the
floor of the House of Commons. But the issue hung on a hair-
trigger throughout Turkey, the Arab States and Israel and
haunted SHAPE headquarters in France, as well as the British
War Office and No. 10 Downing Street.

One has to look backward as well as forward, and frequently
sidewise, in order even to begin to understand the enormous
complexities of this colossally disorganized part of the world.
And this might be a propitious moment for the writer to point
out that the very nexus of this work lies in the crossing and
recrossing of frontiers and in the meeting of peoples at all
hours in all kinds of weather down the years, and especially
during the past year of travel, study and writing. If there
seems to be periodic confusion, the reader may console himself with the knowledge that many of the situations were
hopelessly confusing at the time to almost everybody concerned. There will be frequent paragraphs and even chapters

to stitch up or nail down the sequences of time and events. There are entire libraries of moldering volumes by well-meaning anthropologists, archaeologists, geologists and journeymen travelers who worked themselves into exhaustion and neuroses trying to capsulate, tag and file for public consumption the utterly mercurial, uncontainable phantasmagoria that is the Middle East. The bibliography on this book, alone, would fill a good-sized study.

This bibliography, however, was not annotated for research and footnotes, indices and cross-indexing. It was absorbed on trains, in planes and in filthy fly-ridden hostels and rest houses, broken-down hotels, in desert *wadis* and trenches and a thousand-and-one other places where one does much of the inevitable, interminable waiting that is an ineluctable part of life in the Middle East. This is my story, the way I saw it and the way I see it, and I long, long ago accepted the credo of Walter Duranty and *I write as I please*.

To come to an understanding of how Anglo-American unity could all but destroy itself in this vital area where unity is so paramount, one has to have the working knowledge of the preceding chapters and a consuming curiosity about the stuff of things to come. In a word, the Middle East is going the way of the Far East with terrifying velocity, and largely because of an almost total lack of British-American planning and understanding and coordination of detail on all levels—political, economic, social and military. And if the Middle East goes under the engulfing tide of Russian Communism, future historians can roll up not only the map of Europe but the charts of all mid-Asia and Africa, and start making indentations and marginalia signifying the beginning of the end in the Western Hemisphere.

Some historians of the past and present, with anthropolog-

[49]

ical data to bolster their briefs, seek to trace the darkening twilight of Western power and influence right back to the Middle Ages and beyond. The simple fact is that most of our Anglo-Saxon ancestors were still braining each other with clubs and living a hand-to-mouth existence in caves and hovels when the ancestral peoples of the Middle East were spinning and weaving, writing poetry and fashioning a culture that truly made the Mediterranean "The Cradle of Civilization."

The present emergency actually began less than a hundred years ago. British trade and colonialism already had carried the seeds of its own destruction into India. With the opening of the Suez Canal, after ten violent years of intrigue, murder and herculean labor, the foreshortened trade route to the East brought an inevitable backwash of misfits, ne'er-do-wells, remittance men and cutthroats. This riffraff washed up at Suez and Port Said and drifted into Cairo and along the eastern Mediterranean, the Levant. The pickings were good and the living was easy. Labor was cheap and ignorant. There were spices and oils, cotton and wool aplenty, lumber and fruit, exotic liquors, women—and *opium.*

Opium and hashish boomed the picturesque little fishing villages into sizable seaports. From Greece's Piraeus and old Constantinople to Alexandretta (present-day Iskenderun, now in Turkish Hatay), to Beirut and Haifa, stinking Port Said and Alexandria, the drug trade flourished. Britannia ruled the waves and her lusty, brawling traders prowled off their barkentines and square-riggers to seize fabulous cargoes of drugs, wines and liquors, jewels and women, oils and spices, lumber and wool and the fabulous fruits of the Levant. The Arabic populaces were deliberately debauched. British gold bought and sold emirates and sheikhdoms. Where bribery failed, violence worked. The British sowed their hurricane with profligate hand.

Trade, as always, caused trouble. The French had a foot in the Middle Eastern door in Syria. And they had the free-booting Foreign Legion, the dregs of the deserters, escapees, murderers, perverts of a dozen countries—the real *élite* of the Legion—to do the bidding of Paris and Marseilles. Even as trouble started, however, between the British and the French, Gallic logic and British greed came to an understanding. There was loot enough for all. The Anglo-French conspiracy for nearly half a century was to divide and rule the incredible riches of the Levant.

Both powers, however, prudently boosted their garrison strength in the Levant. The British rescued Egypt in the Sudanese uprising, and stayed on. Trouble-shooting garrisons were stationed permanently at the terminal points and along the isthmus of Suez. And the mighty British fleet now patrolled the Mediterranean, guns bristling, to cow any Islamic sultan imprudent enough to demur against the invasion from the West.

It took World War I to drive home to the British and the French the enormous strategic value of the Levant, Meso-potamia (present-day Iraq), and the value in sheer cannon fodder of the fierce, warlike but ignorant Arabs. Allenby's campaign in Palestine and the fabled exploits of T. E. Law-rence of Arabia are thrice-told tales and need no repetition in this thumbnail background to the current emergency. Suffice it that World War I, like any great conflagration, stirred the stuff of revolt and revolution, the smoldering discontent that flared into violence and bloodshed.

Those bloody and perfidious postwar years were the cli-mactic years for both the British and the French, their common point-of-no-return with honor. While the Jewish peoples struggling for a homeland in Palestine were fobbed off and traduced by shameless British deception, Arab demonstrations for liberty were put down with a savagery and violence almost unmatched in British colonial history. With a callousness and arrogance unmatched even by the pukka sahibs and the Bengal Lancers of India, the British colonial regiments and their ultimate bosses, the High Commissioners, sealed the ultimate fate of the Briton in the Middle East.

Intrigue in the desert reached its all-time high during the quarter century when Britain began in earnest to exploit the real gold, the thick black gold, which already was trickling from the ooze in the sandy soil of "Old Mess-pot," Iraq. Drillers in Iran had hit the jackpot. If the geologists and the oil engineers were right, and they speedily proved they were, here was wealth beyond all imagining in an endless oil sea which could be piped to water outlets and shipped around the earth. With a refinery in a strategic location and a mighty tanker fleet to take the oil, the little Anglo-Iranian Oil Company began its miraculous growth which was to make it the most powerful single oil corporation in the entire world, with the world's largest refinery at Abadan and the world's largest tanker fleet, comprising Great Britain's single largest overseas investment—and the Frankenstein monster which was to smite its master in 1951.

It was just at the turn of the century, fifty-two years ago, that the Anglo-Iranian colossus was born. Winston Churchill examined the extensive reports from William Knox D'Arcy who had already begun to exploit Iranian oil under a sixty-year concession from the impoverished Persian government. Parliament appropriated two million pounds to give the British government a controlling interest in the project, and to insure

[52]

fuel oil for the great new British war fleet of the future. Since 1828, Czarist Russia had dominated Persian trade—wool, furs, raw cotton, Persian rugs and silver and a caviar monopoly still maintained by the Kremlin. A Czarist trade mission in 1907 signed an agreement which gave Britain a virtual monopoly on southern Iranian trade. Twenty-seven years later, with Anglo-Iranian booming, the British jammed through a new sixty-year lease entitling them to drilling and oil exploitation over some 16 per cent of Iranian territory.

Communist Russia took an increasingly dim view of British expansion in Iran. Russia was and is oil-hungry and her fields at Batum and Baku and the Baku refinery are still considered too vulnerable to attack from the south through Turkey and northern Iran. Under Russian prodding greedy old Shah Reza Khan—Mohammed Reza's father—began mutterings about an upward revision of oil royalties and a downward revision of British income taxes. The Shah himself, of course, was fabulously wealthy and with the rich and landed aristocracy was seeking merely to swell his fortunes. The Iranian peasantry lived and live in unimaginable, filthy squalor and hunger.

Danger signals were flashing with increasing frequency through the middle thirties. British policy ignored them with lofty indifference. If American policy-makers had the vaguest notion that this far-distant heat lightning presaged violent storm, they gave no hint. Aside from an occasional archaeologist pottering about in the Iranian hinterlands, Iran remained as remote as Afghanistan or Tibet.

The outbreak of World War II in the West apparently obliterated any top-level Middle Eastern thinking in Britain or the United States. Plans, if any, for the stormy future of Iran were expunged, although the puzzling *Sitzkrieg* gave ample time for Middle Eastern experts in Whitehall and Washington to survey their territory anew.

It required the smashing *Blitzkrieg* and the fall of France with the consequent collapse of the French Armies of the Levant in Syria to focus high-level attention once more upon Iran and the Middle East. Winston Churchill moved with stealthy haste and the pitiful resources at his command to dam the disastrous gaps in the Balkans and in stubborn neutral Turkey, the logical springboards for the Axis leap into the unprotected Levant. Axis agents swarmed through the Balkans and Turkey and into Syria and Iraq and Iran, aided and abetted by their Communist allies (the Nazi-Soviet pact of 1939 had reached full flower). Egypt's Italian colony in Cairo funneled reams of precise military intelligence data to Rome, whence it was promptly relayed to the Italian columns advancing across Cyrenaica in the Western Desert upon Alexandria. And the restive Arab populations of Trans-Jordan and Saudi Arabia began to receive smuggled rifles and high explosives from German and Communist agents and from the underground storehouses of the Grand Mufti of Jerusalem and his terrorist aide, Fawzi el-Kaukji, who was busily organizing the treacherous Arab renegades who joined the Vichy French forces to seize Beirut, Damascus and the Baghdad airdrome. Ensuing events of the next perilous year are fairly familiar history to anyone who followed the desperate fighting in the Middle East, although many of the lesser-known happenings will be covered in detail in later chapters.

The essential point, for the sake of clarity and straight historical continuity here, is that for the first time since the U. S. Marines had dashed dramatically to "the shores of Tripoli" (in 1804, to rescue an American citizen), officers and enlisted men of the U. S. armed forces entered the Middle East. No official units were involved. The United States was not yet at war and would not be until the following December 7th. But the U. S. Army rushed "observers," tank specialists, intelligence officers and enlisted aides to follow the Western Desert fighting and the Syrian campaign of General Sir Henry Maitland ("Jumbo") Wilson.

It was the first time since 1918 that British and American officers had stood together on a battlefront, and history to all intents and purposes unhappily began to repeat itself.

First, many of the American "observers" and "experts" were cocksure, overbearing and openly contemptuous of the battered British Eighth Army which was taking its first pounding from Rommel's deadly *Afrikakorps*. The British withdrawals from Greece and Crete still rankled, particularly in the breasts of the Australians and the New Zealanders who had survived these two disasters, and scoffing American newcomers were considered well-nigh unbearable.

The scornful attitudes of many of these American officers and enlisted men were insufferable to this writer as well. As war correspondents many of the journalists now with the Eighth Army had seen fighting since Ethiopia and Spain, in Western Europe and the Balkans and Middle East, and the spectacle of a handful of unblooded Yanks—visiting firemen, no less—demeaning the desperate British was nauseating. It became downright sickening when the U. S. tank "experts" grandiosely delivered the first shipment of our high-turreted General Lee tanks. These under-gunned, slow, waddling deathtraps had been rushed by convoys under forced draught halfway round the world and up the Suez Canal to help stop the seemingly invincible Rommel. British tank crews took them reluctantly into battle. The carnage was awful. The General Lee tank was an engineering monstrosity. It was pitifully slow and its narrow treads sank deep in the desert sands, rendering the tank virtually unmaneuverable. The interior design was impossible and the cooling system a flop. But the outrageously idiotic feature of the General Lee was its weird, high gun-and-observation turret mounted, like the bridge on an aircraft carrier, on the starboard side. Manifestly, the Lee could not take a hull-down position. For those uninitiated in desert warfare, the fighting in the desert was uncannily like combat at sea. A ship, hull-down on the horizon, presents little or no target. In the desert, a tank, hull-down in a *wadi* or depression, can fire, "submerge" and emerge to fire again, with a maximum of protection from the terrain.

The high-turreted Lees were blasted into blazing infernos by the rapid-firing high-muzzle-velocity fire of the vicious, underslung German Tigers, and by the first of the deadly 88's introduced in the Western Desert. Small wonder that the first contingents of American advisers to the British Eighth Army became somewhat less than welcome on the fronts and in rear echelon areas.

However, Cairo itself was another story and in the steaming, noisome, fly-ridden Egyptian capital, the British colonial and the professional British rear echelon officer were as insolent, toplofty and domineering as only the practiced British snob can be. The funk-holes of the Continental-Savoy and Shepheard's Hotel were thick with well-pressed and manicured, tonsured and shining young officers who spent their mornings over paper work and their afternoons in dalliance on the terrace, in the bar and elsewhere with the abundantly available young women of the Cairo colony. Cairo stank, literally and figuratively, for the duration of the war, and the moral effluvia was never more offensive than at Shepheard's, the Continental, the swank, plush Gezirah Club—cricket and tennis daily and tea promptly at four o'clock.

Bearded, exhausted, sweat-stained young commandos of the gallant British Long Range Desert Patrols would stumble into Shepheard's and stalk out again to seek billets anywhere, rather than rub elbows with the dandied officers who haunted the place. Small wonder that Shepheard's and the swank Turf Club were the first targets of outraged Egyptian rioters, the "Buluks" (auxiliary police) in the January fighting.

Officially there was a pained politeness and the fiction of good will and general agreement at top levels among the British and the Americans, with open mutual contempt and even hatred just below. These, however, were surface impressions. The ever-present chasm dividing the British and the Americans goes much deeper.

7

ISRAEL OVERSHADOWS and permeates the low-pressure area of the stormy Middle East like a freakish and unexpected typhoon. Jewish nationalism collided, in 1946, with the dead epicenter of earth-quaking Arab nationalism in the Levant, staggered the complacent British colonials with its violence, and shocked—even horrified—wealthy Zionists in America who had been "fighting" a war of independence under dead syntax with fountain pens and checkbooks, but with only the foggiest notion of what the Palestine storm really was all about. Isolated in an Arabic sand-sea of hatred, "the bile of envy and the froth of fear," the desperate Jewry of Palestine at last struck out in all directions with all the hoarded small arms and dynamite at their command. Here in Palestine were reckless, hopeless men and women and their children with everything to win and absolutely nothing to lose. Behind them lay their ancestors, drawn and quartered, tortured, gassed and burned, or used, like guinea pigs, to establish at what point human

[58]

resistance crumples against intolerable heat, sub-zero cold or the "bends" of oxygen chambers.

To an Irishman, the Jewish explosion was a joy to behold, especially since this writer had been *sic'd* on to stories, through the World War II years, which editorial policy of the *New York Times* had deemed too hot for a Jewish correspondent to handle. It might be pertinent to mention that these dispatches included the murderous anti-Jewish operations of Fawzi el-Kaukji, the deposed Grand Mufti Haj Amin el Husseini, Rashid Ali el Gaylani, and the cold-blooded British lower-echelon operatives who conveniently "lost" certificates which would have permitted thousands of miserable, starving, dispossessed Jews to emigrate via Istanbul and the Dardanelles to Palestine. These Jewish refugees were shipped back to the tender mercies of Gestapo operatives in Bulgaria and Romania, or perished in the leaky tubs they chartered to transport themselves and their families toward the haven of Palestine.

These horrendous events split the British and the Americans in the Middle East and elsewhere. Despite the fact that Hebrew refugees were enlisting to fight wherever possible on all fronts in Syria, on commando raids in the Aegean islands and in the Western Desert, the British attitude was one of almost supreme disregard for ultimate Jewish aims in the Middle East. Outwardly—that is, from the State Department— the American attitude was negative and cautious. The hard news, however, ultimately got home, as it almost inevitably does. It blew the top off Zionist organizations in America for a time. It gravely disturbed top-level planning for the far-distant, political fate of the Jews in the Middle East. It riffled, and almost exposed, the sell-out of Poland and Polish Jewry and the long-suppressed and horrifying story of the slaughter in the Warsaw ghetto of that city's starveling but defiant Jewish population. For a time it almost forced an inquiry into the Katyn Forest massacre of 15,000 Polish officers and upper-grade non-coms. The combination of these events almost blew a fuse on the San Francisco Conference in May, 1945. To this writer's certain knowledge, Anthony Eden was so outraged by Russian arrogance in the kidnaping of the Polish Government at the outset of the U.N. Charter conference that he cabled London for permission to boycott the conference until the Poles were released or accounted for.

Back came the word: "Proceed." And from the White House, still reeling and rocking under the impact of Roosevelt's death, came the word: "Proceed." Stassen and Vandenberg attended San Francisco, along with John Foster Dulles, as Republican "watchdogs," but they had been carefully tethered on trusteeships and procedural issues at remote distances from the real dogfight over major issues.

The issues were never joined. The demand for Israel's independence was sidetracked, along with the smothered protests of the disfranchised Poles, the Serbs of Yugoslavia, the Chinese, and the small but strident voices of representatives from the Baltic States, who sought to remind the U.N. founders that after all Latvia, Esthonia and Lithuania had been disfranchised too.

It looked like touch and go for a time. Actually the issues were never in doubt. The agenda had been written, in extremely fine print, and the skids were greased. Subcommittee and committee chairmen slid through prearranged debate, waving prearranged and mimeographed paragraphs to the sacred charter. Alger Hiss gaveled the seconding motions and the votings. Trygve Lie droned the results. San Francisco and the U.N. Charter were consigned to a pigeonhole in infamous

[60]

history. Harry Truman flew out from Washington to set the seal on the most ignominious surrender to naked tyranny since the Munich of '38.

The Western sellout was virtually complete. Poland, since January, 1942, had been consigned to oblivion by the notorious deal which partitioned the Polish state between Nazi Germany and Communist Russia. Czechoslovakia was doomed. Hungary, Romania and Bulgaria were earmarked for the Soviet orbit. Mihailovich of Yugoslavia was abandoned and the Communist Tito was exalted at San Francisco as the democratic messiah of the Balkans. The Arab States, led by the Arab League and a particularly vehement Yemen, slunk along.

The order of the day was expediency. It worked. It worked, that is, upon the stylized and ramiform floor of the San Francisco Civic Opera House and upon the whirling, pungent stencils which stamped and rolled out the doings of this conclave of massive minds intent upon authoritarian order—"an assembly of mice presided over by a few cats." The phrase is Ely Culbertson's.

The end result of San Francisco was a rubber-stamping of the Far Eastern surrender to Communist hegemony and a consignment of the Balkans and Central Europe to Communist domination. The San Francisco Conference merely initialed the ruinous Russian occupation of Berlin and the partition of Austria. That damage already had been done, over the vigorous wartime protests of Eisenhower. In theory, it loosely consigned the Mediterranean basin to British dominance and continued their exploitation of the riches of the Middle East.

In practice it did no such thing. The truculent, disorganized Arabs went home to think over the nothingness they had salvaged from the glamour, the endless champagne, the phony obeisance and politesse they had received at San Francisco. And the women. All the gains were distinctly evanescent.

The desperate, nearly bankrupt British had gained time. The Socialist Government under Attlee had a temporary lease on life, until the tinsel of San Francisco tarnished and the ineluctable issues appeared once more to haunt the War and Foreign Offices.

For the Hebrew peoples, however, the entire procedure of the vaunted San Francisco Conference had acted as a kind of emetic. It smelled foully of Geneva and Lausanne at the close of World War I. There was the stench of treachery and betrayal. It required no extensive intelligence service, although the Israel's Sûreté is fairly good, to ascertain that the British already were smuggling fresh arms to the Arabs, heavily in Syria and Egypt, and briefing the British-controlled Arab Legion on the Jewish underground.

Israel's Irgun struck first. The Irgun Zvai Leumi—Hebrew for "National Military Organization"—chopped into the tough but thin-spread British forces in Palestine. Dynamite, captured British Sten guns and rifles, grenades and hangings—"an eye for an eye and a tooth for a tooth"—were brought into play against the British. The campaign, led by Menachem Begin, a Polish Soviet Jew who had escaped from Russia, began to pay off. Begin had no house room for the fainthearted, the compromisers, or even the recognized authorities of the Jewish Agency, which theoretically controlled Jewish resistance policy in Palestine. Irony of the entire campaign was that Begin was harassed by the Haganah, the official arm of the Jewish Agency, even as he fought tooth and nail against the tough, savage and unrelenting British Palestinian police. With a price of ten thousand British pounds on his head, Begin and his desperate men went on fighting, amalgamating and fighting again. Menachem Begin was no breast-beater but a doer.

Menachem Begin has told his own story in *The Revolt*, a 386-page narrative of his operations with the Irgun, and this writer has no intention of stealing the thunder and hyperbole of his story. Indeed, knowing the Middle East, none could doubt that Begin's story, give a little, take a little, is actually accurate. The inside story of the Irgun is bloody, romantic, alternately sordid and wildly heroic, and will be touched on later.

The main point here is that that embattled, struggling Israel, with a population of a million and a half Jews, musters an army today of nearly 90,000 extremely tough, well-trained and fanatical young Hebrews schooled in the hazardous art of street and desert fighting, full of gutter cunning, and blooded in the short-lived war with the Arab League. The fact that the Israelis bested it in the Gaza hostilities is no criterion. Arabs are extremely good fighting men, indeed, when well led, well armed and with something to fight for, be it a holy cause, arms, loot or women.

Israel has two great internal problems—the economic and the age-old mutual suspicion of Jew against Jew. Israel is desperately poor, and without the American crutch of financial support would collapse in a figurative tomorrow—an obviously impossible catastrophe in the light of the deep-burning determination of world Jewry to keep Israel a national state. Many a ditch must be dug for imperative irrigation and many a crop planted before Israel can even begin to support the awful weight of the immigration of European Jewry which threatens to boost the Israeli population to 2,000,000 before 1953.

Israel's second problem is the gravest. A visitor to Israel is astonished to find that Oriental Jews hate Western European Jews. The deadly hatred of Polish and German and Central European Jews for each other is incredible until one has met it. And chauvinism: To speak any language save Hebrew in Tel Aviv or Haifa is to leave oneself open to scorn or obvious contumely. Young Jewish buckos prowl the streets—like the *Kurfuerstendam* under Hitler?—or Yorkville in New York?—seeking even an implausible pretext for combat against the *Auslander*.

More jaws have been broken of late in Israel for this reason. This is unhealthy, unhappy and totally unnecessary. In the first place, no one goes to Israel without a thorough screening. The investigation of one's papers and background reminds one of a totalitarian state. So does the "tail" attached to any foreign journalist the moment he enters the country. Obviously, these are outward manifestations of growing nationalistic pains—yet they take a terrible toll in otherwise neutral sentiment. The trend of the world at large is toward a genuine support of an independent Israel. It is not only in America that man supports the underdog.

In Israel chauvinism is going too far. Entering Israel as an independent journalist, a writer is subjected to a screening comparable only to the days of Hitler Germany. Or Russia today. In this tiny but dynamic state there is a complete intolerance for any written or spoken word that might be construed as pro-Arab—as, in most of the Arab states, any sympathy toward Israel is lese majesty. A simple observation that Britain has a Gargantuan problem in dealing with the Middle East is regarded as a diatribe against Israel. The suggestion that Zionism has propped Israel against the rising, hammering tides of Arab nationalism and xenophobia is viewed as heresy—although most Israelis hate the necessary charity from the United States.

David Ben-Gurion, Israel's outspoken Prime Minister, aroused the wrath of American Zionists with a recent candid examination of the vagaries of Zionist organizations around the world.

Ben-Gurion obviously meant no harm. He was sniping for internal and political consumption against such sans-culottes as Menachem Begin, Parliamentary leader of the Herut, or "Freedom" party. (Begin is still raising hell with the moderates to expand Israel across the Jordan.) These forensics would be forgotten almost as quickly as they are uttered, if there were not the ever-present Arab problem, and the encroachment of the Communists. Sleeping in both beds, the Communists glean a close knowledge of the political bed habits of the combatants. And the Communists use this knowledge to the nth of its advantage.

The end is not nearly yet. The internal and external problems of the Israeli state and the roiling ocean of Arab nationalism about its borders presage a sea change that can only lead to a temporary lull in the storm—or a change that will strike at the very foundations of the emergency sea walls and jetties erected to stem the tide of erosive, disruptive nationalism that will sweep away forever the Western barriers to a flood tide of Communism in the Middle East.

8

Born in hatred and suckled on austerity and adversity, the Israeli state is in its fifth year of troubled existence between the devilish problems of Arab xenophobia, Communism, divergent Anglo-American policies, and the deep blue Mediterranean. Miraculously, the tiny, triangular nation set amid the Arabic land sea continues to bob up, corklike, from each new rolling comber threatening its existence.

Unless and until Anglo-American statesmanship brings order out of the current chaos in the political Middle East, the deadliest threat to Israel's life and sovereignty would seem to lie in the seething uncertainties of the Arab states upon her borders: Lebanon and Syria on the north, Jordan at the center and in the south, Saudi Arabia and Egypt to the south and west. Actually, the fate of Israel and her explosive neighbors seems far more likely to be settled over polished conference tables at the State Department in Washington, in stormy policy sessions in Whitehall, in board rooms of gigantic interlocking oil companies in England, Holland and America, and in the crenelated towers of the Kremlin.

The inexorable march of events throws harsh but realistic light upon the current fate of small nations caught up in the maelstrom of hard-boiled power politics. *Peace,* so desperately needed by Israel to shore up her rickety economy, inevitably will be denied the Jewish National State as long as the Arabs are convinced that they must expect more trickery and double-dealing from London and Washington. *Time,* an absolute necessity if Israeli economy is to accomplish the miraculous transition from agriculture to industry, and still maintain the agriculture imperative to her eventual self-support—time will run out unless the Israeli state can rely on something beyond the hated charity of American Jewry and establish *credits* based upon sound, building Israeli collateral, and not the fickle, emotional, highly political absentee landlordism which many Israelis feel wields a malignant influence upon the government offices in Jerusalem and Tel Aviv. This landlordism is deeded in dollars extracted in a multiple thousand of fund drives and campaigns in America and dedicated to the eventual super-imposition, like a strait jacket, of the strangling fetters of theocracy upon the struggling Jewish National State.

Israel's deadliest enemies recognize the Religious Bloc as their truest Fifth Column. After all, it is an inbred and backward-looking defeatism and passive resistance which, vastly more than Western imperialism and colonialism, locked the wheels of social and economic progress for the world of Islam. And it is a black and bitter irony, indeed, that atheistic Communists and small but powerful policy cliques in Whitehall and Washington find themselves playing a companion role in furthering the smothering of Israel's progress to power and international comity.

Premier David Ben-Gurion is all too sensitively aware of this menace. So, for that matter, is Foreign Minister Moshe Sharett, Israel's able U. S. Ambassador, and U.N. Chief Delegate Aubrey (Abba) Eban, and General Yagil Yadin, Commander in Chief of the Israeli Army. Israel's leaders are, simultaneously, sadly cognizant that they are hamstrung in the forging of a truly democratic Jewish national homeland and national state and reduced to something approaching authoritarian rule, while bowing to the rituals and fetishes of a Jewish religious bloc which plays directly into the myriad arms of the enemy.

Like it or not, there are cold-blooded men within and without the British and United States Governments who would come to terms on any figurative tomorrow with Arab leaders, sacrificing Israeli independence on the altar of expediency. It is symptomatic that these men occupy positions of power in politics and business and the limitless areas of international trade. Within their ranks, they include otherwise respected and able financiers, scholars-*cum*-advisers in government, insular up-from-the-ranks politicians, Communist or pro-Communist fellow-travelers dedicated, as ever, to the advancement of Soviet expansionism; hard-cased and hard-handed oil engineers and timorous peace-at-any-price adherents, and, of course, a frothy spattering of anti-Semitic lunatic fringers. It is likewise symptomatic that very nearly all of these extraordinary individuals found themselves aligned with Hitler during the heyday of the Nazi-Soviet pact of 1939, and in outraged opposition to Nazi Germany following what was described as the perfidy of the German attack upon Communist Russia.

It is *not* symptomatic, but as shocking and revolting as the open exposure of the diseased tissue itself, that this clique of conscienceless, international racketeers has pervaded the very roots of Western governments in a relentless, eleventh-hour attempt to balk Western rearmament, the North Atlantic Treaty Organization, a Middle East Command; to spike and brake laggard United Nations action toward unified resistance to Soviet aggression, and to pave the highroad for step-by-step Soviet hegemony over the entire Middle East.

Why Israel, then—as a catalyst? The simple answer is that Israel is a special kind of microcosm in the enormous crucible of the Middle East. Israel is a test case of the sincerity and the intentions of the West, as opposed to the floundering, uncertain Arab peoples and the all-too-murderous certainties of the Russians.

Unhappily, the Israelis themselves constitute a peculiar and uncertain compound. As the Israeli population creeps toward 2,000,000 (sometime in late '52 or early '53), the very components of the state may change. This is a risk carefully calculated by Ben-Gurion and his uneasy, bedeviled ministers. Despite the most rigorous screening, the waves of immigrants into Israel contain men and women dedicated to the eventual anarchical overthrow of the Israeli government and the establishment of a desperate Communist state in the heartland of Middle East. Israel's swelling population is drawn from Central and Eastern European areas where Communism alone afforded the organization and arms enabling limited resistance to the former enemy.

None of the foregoing is meant to imply that the Israeli state is a growing, ticking time bomb in the Middle East epicenter. What I mean is that Communist infiltration into Israel has been considerable, and is continuing.

Turkey has been an extremely fallow field for Communist operatives. All Arab states, with the possible exception of Iran and Egypt, are constitutionally—in the physical sense—armored against the encroachments of Communist dialectics. The misery and the disfranchisements are there, but the organizational network, even with the aid and assistance of the former Grand Mufti, leaves something to be desired, from the point of view of the Kremlin.

In Israel, at least, there is a deep and basic conspiratorial organization of resistance to any attack from *without*. Israel's population is composed of emotional, violent, sometimes reckless and altogether anxious and suspicious peoples bred on idealism, sabotage, smuggled small arms, illegal immigration and what seemed at the time of the glorious revolution to be a war against the world. This is ripe soil for Communism, the attack from *within*.

The attack is under way.

The Israeli attitude toward the Arabs is one of basic contempt. That the Arabs have inspired and merited the attitude is of no immediate matter to Communist operatives in Israel. It is being exploited from both ends.

The Israeli attitude toward the British is one of fear and deep-laid hatred, intermingled with a sense of triumph that events have conspired to render the British hoist on their own petard.

The Israeli attitude toward Americans is almost hopelessly muddled, and with reasonably good reason. Americans, generally, are regarded as rather Pandora-like peoples who helped, monetarily, to lift the lid on the box and are now horrified by the swarm of troubles unleashed. It might be added that the visitations of Americans to Israel have done little to dispel this idea. It is infuriating to the Israelis that sympathetic and benevolent Americans fly and sail out, in hundreds of thousands, to visit their country and seek, literally and figuratively, to pat the state and its peoples upon the head. Speeches are made and dedications thrive, but the visiting firemen ultimately take ship or plane to go home and recount their adventures, and the deadly business of mere survival in Israel goes on. It matters less than nothing to the stalwart, chauvinistic young Israeli pioneer from a Polish concentration camp that a kindly old lady from the Bronx or Dubuque weeps copious tears over the emergence of a Jewish homeland, especially if she seems to take a kind of parental pride in the boy. He is uncomfortable, impatient and wishes that the old lady would take herself off. It must be added that this is an attitude unlimited in the world, whether it concerns guerrilla troops subjected to VIP's, GI's in Korea, or bedridden wounded in base hospitals.

In Israel, it is doubly insufferable, for here the Israeli trooper usually knows what he fought for, and for how long, and after what intolerable indignities in Germany, Poland, Romania, Hungary, Bulgaria, Yugoslavia or elsewhere.

Israeli intransigence goes far deeper than the trooper confronted by the old lady. While Israel is ready and willing to enter into a Middle Eastern alliance with the Western Big Three Powers and Turkey, the Israelis want some very definite answers to some extremely definite questions. Israel's 90,000-man combat army, with a 200,000-man potential, can and will be committed to general Middle Eastern defense, *provided:*

(1) The West offers concrete proof that the entire Middle East will be defended. Like the Turks, the Israelis are realistic. They are not convinced that Anglo-American unity is as solid and unshakable as presented in the diplomatic façades at Paris and Rome.

(2) Western appeasement of the Arab states ceases forthwith. The mysterious and labyrinthine U. S. policy in Iran, according to the Israelis, needs further explanation. If Mos-

sadegh of Iran receives a bulwarking loan, why? How many commitments (at Israel's expense) have been undertaken to insure the U. S. monies to Iran?

(3) Israel's alliance to the Middle East Command is not overpublicized. The Israelis are perfectly content to fight, and fight well, alongside the West, if Israel's commitments are not made a political football in the arena of Middle East politicking.

(4) Finally, that considerable fresh economic aid be proffered to Israel immediately. Israel's defense program, combined with the internal problems of mere survival, are a great drain—Israel's trade balance with the contiguous Arab states, her logical trade partners, is almost nonexistent—and Israel needs dollars for international exchange.

There is a further plus to the Israeli unhappiness over Anglo-American plans, if that is the word, for the Middle East. The Israeli leaders are definitely queasy lest some new top-level, "over-all strategy" supersede the rather weird U.N., bi- and tri-lateral agreements reached or initialed at Paris in 1952. The Israelis have very little tolerance for any further Big Three or Big Four talks, anywhere. In this attitude, they reflect the considered opinion of the stalwart Turks—much closer to the Israelis than is commonly suspected—and certain Arab states, including the Lebanon and Saudi Arabia.

The wooing of the Arab League is definitely disturbing to the Israeli Foreign Office.

A leading spokesman for the Israelis told this correspondent last winter as the State Department reshuffled its diplomatic corps in the Middle East: "Your people in America are tethering the wrong camel. Arab philosophy in wartime is abundantly clear. If you are weak, you do not deserve Arab support. If you are strong, you don't need it. It is best, therefore, to wait until the last moment to see who is weak and who is strong."

In a word, strange as it sounds and seems, Turkey and Israel seem fated to some kind of mutual, limited alliance which is calculated to impel a further, limited alliance from the Arabs at some distant date.

All, or most, of the foregoing begs one fundamental question: British policy vis-à-vis the Arab League, especially Hashemite Jordan and Egypt. Willy-nilly, the British usually have been able to buffer their tenuous Middle Eastern position by the playing-off of Arab greeds and jealousies, dynastic ambitions and, more recently, oil royalties. These tactics are wearing thin, for the lowliest shiekhs are fond of exhibiting their latest contracts with the British and Americans, and the camaraderie born of mutual wealth is assuaging age-old tribal misunderstandings and blood feuds.

The sober, considered feeling throughout the Middle East is that the Syrian-Israeli dispute over "aggression" in the Lake Huleh region is being given artificial respiration merely as a bargaining point. Neither side in the Huleh "fighting" is severely exercised about it, despite the deaths of a handful of Israelis and Syrians in border sniping.

The spectre of Israeli expansionism is a much larger ghost and bogy according to the Syrians and their Arabic neighbors. The Arabs charge that Israeli nationalists have definite designs on the lands beyond the Jordan. The Syrians are especially vehement about this, although Colonel Adib Shishakly, the Syrian strong man, has risked again and again a threatened bullet from assassins as the price of negotiation and mediation by U.N. observers.

[73]

Inexperienced and desperately self-conscious, the Israeli leaders are seeking to meet in the embarrassingly public gold-fish bowls of international conferences the sticky questions of Israel's ambitions for the future. Ben-Gurion cannot ignore the almost universal appeal of the still-heroic Menachem Begin and his expansionist Herut party which would move here and now against the common, considered enemy, the Arabs.

Neither can Ben-Gurion ignore, at home, the very real centrist sentiment for peace, time and credits, and the categorical imperative of his peoples, be they left, centrist or rightist.

Israelis live today on the bare fringe of existence, eating the shards of bitter economy and surrounded by a hostile and un-understanding world. Home life and business life are chaotic. Communications are virtually nonexistent. Travel is terribly expensive and uncertain. Food is hard to come at and dreadfully dear. Israel's climate is excessively hot (perhaps a blessing in winter), but anathema to agricultural experts wound up in irrigation projects. Eggs are three per week, on the ration, and meat a quarter-pound—try and get it. Bread and cheese is the normal diet in the middle-class home.

Yet the peoples of Israel thirst for music, poetry and art. Their appetite for culture is insatiable. The Israel Philharmonic Orchestra is sold out tenfold, and concerts are repeated ad infinitum.

Israel's fund of diplomats, economic experts, solid politicos is threadbare. That she has managed to keep her head above water is close to miraculous.

Is it worth it? The Israelis seem to think so. The austerity and adversity seem to breed rugged peoples. Israel lives, thrives and expands, economically and politically. Israel is a constant threat to British colonial arrogance and American indifference in the Middle East, and a divisive influence between them.

9

A KNIFE-EDGED BOOMERANG, unpredictable Hashemite Jordan lies restively along the central and southern frontiers of hated Israel, bordering the Egyptian Sinai, Saudi Arabia, Iraq and Syria, and—boomerang-like—constitutes a whirling, thrusting threat to the unsteady equilibrium of the Middle East. King Tallal I rules strategic Jordan's 34,750 miles and its 1,500,000 Arab population with an unsteady but merciless hand. A prey to sudden rages and darkling fears, the forty-one-year-old Hashemite monarch seized the Jordanian throne late last summer following the murder in a Jerusalem mosque of his fabled father, King Abdullah ibn Hussein, a sixty-nine-year-old thirty-ninth-generation direct descendant of the Prophet through his daughter Fatima.

Abdullah's murder struck the world of Islam like the crack of doom. While he was both hated and feared by Arab fanatics, including the conscienceless Haj Amin el Husseini, the ex-Grand Mufti of Jerusalem, Abdullah had been an anchor man

[76]

in the Middle East. He was known to have been grooming his younger, second son, Naif, a pleasure-loving thirty-seven-year-old, but Allah willed it otherwise.

Thirteen major Arab and political leaders of the Moslem world have been assassinated in six years. With the possible exception of the slaying on March 7, 1951 of Premier General Ali Razmara of Iran—the murder which touched off the Anglo-Iranian oil struggle—no other killing could have had such immediate and long-range effects upon the fate of the Levant and Islam as that of Abdullah.

Abdullah was a dreamer, but a doer too. Born in the holy Moslem city of Mecca in 1882, he reached young manhood still a subject of the hated Ottoman Empire which bestrode all Araby. His father, Hussein ibn Ali, a patriarch in the ancient desert clan of the Hashemites, was a *sherif* under appointment from Constantinople. Young Abdullah was ambitious, but he seemed fated to continued frustration.

The outbreak of the first World War found Abdullah negotiating with the legendary T. E. Lawrence of Arabia. He helped to lead and inspire the Arab revolt against the Turks and he fought bloodily and at times gallantly, emerging from the desert campaigns as a leading contender for one of the Arab kingdoms which were established in what used to be Mesopotamia and the rolling, richer deserts and plateaus to the south. It was Abdullah's father, however, who drew the throne of the Hejaz, in the highlands off the northeastern coast of the Red Sea. Abdullah's younger brother, Feisal, was named king of Syria in an Anglo-French compromise, and Abdullah finally was crowned king of Iraq. Then the French under their League of Nations mandate decided to depose Feisal, and Abdullah had to step down in Iraq for his younger brother. Bitter and disillusioned, he drifted back into the Hejaz to lead his father's armies against the invading forces of King Ibn Saud of Saudi Arabia. In a swift but bloody desert campaign, Abdullah was defeated and forced to flee as his father was exiled and the Hejaz came under the expanding dynasty of Saud.

It was at this time that the triumphant Western powers began in earnest to appreciate and exploit the wealth and strategic value of the sprawling Middle Eastern lands and waterways. Winston Churchill undertook one of his many field trips into the Levant, interrupting Abdullah's plans for a new Syrian campaign. Churchill offered Abdullah the Emirate of Trans-Jordan under a British mandate.

Trans-Jordan was no bargain, but to the ambitious little prince it was the beginning of a kingdom and a steppingstone to his lifelong dream of a Greater Syria, incorporating Syria and the Lebanon, Palestine, Iraq and Jordan under the sceptre of a Hashemite ruler. Abdullah swore fealty to the British and with one or two minor exceptions remained steadfastly loyal on all major matters of foreign policy. The British were generous. They paid him nearly $6,000,000 a year to build and strengthen Trans-Jordan, and in 1946 the territory became an independent kingdom under the name of Jordan with Abdullah on the throne. The British had sent out a disarmingly rolypoly British officer to aid Abdullah in the formation and training of Bedouin Arabs in the Arab Legion. Brigadier John Bagot Glubb Pasha did an extraordinary job. Within a few short years, the Arab Legion numbered 15,000 hard-riding, straight-shooting troopers with light but suitable equipment and splendid *esprit de corps*.

The Palestinian partition exploded the short-lived war between Israel and the Arab League. Syria and the Lebanon, Egypt, Saudi Arabia, Iraq and the Yemen made thunderous and ferocious noises of unity and bloodthirstiness, but it was

Jordan's Arab Legion which produced the only real resistance to the fierce Israelis.

Abdullah, an opportunist, and with the tacit blessings of Whitehall, came to a separate peace with Israel and annexed his holdings in Old Jerusalem and Arab Palestine to Jordan. Abdullah then turned back to his dream of a Greater Syria. He paused long enough to put his domestic affairs in order. Prince Tallal, a violent Anglophobe with a personal hatred of Brigadier Glubb Pasha, attacked the Commander in Chief with a revolver. Abdullah sternly sent the young man off to a mental home in Switzerland. The little King of Jordan then embarked (by British plane with another British airliner for his entourage) upon the ambitious but ill-fated trip which was to lead to his assassination some six weeks later in Jerusalem.

King Abdullah readily granted this writer a private audience in his royal suite at the Ankara Palas in Turkey. It is always flattering to a journalist to learn that heads of state and major diplomats have read one's dispatches. King Abdullah had read mine for years in the *New York Times,* he told me, and either his secretariat carried voluminous files or the little monarch had an extraordinarily retentive memory, for he mentioned and quoted from several articles covering the nearby Balkans and the Middle East during the course of World War II.

On the subject of his visit to Turkey at this critical time—the issue of Turkey's admittance to the North Atlantic Treaty Organization still hung in doubt—King Abdullah was disarmingly candid. He admitted high hopes that Turkey would take the diplomatic and military lead in the formation of an Arab-Moslem bloc which might ultimately encompass all Islam, from Morocco and Tunisia through the entire Middle East to Afghanistan, Pakistan and perhaps beyond. He spoke softly and thoughtfully, sitting in a big chair in his flowing black robes and his draped *kaffiyeh,* a white turban, which rested on his broad, untroubled brow. He chain-smoked the fine gold-tipped cigarettes which the Turkish President, Celal Bayar, invariably sends down from his villa to distinguished visitors. And from time to time King Abdullah looked out of the large double windows and across the balcony toward the Turkish Parliament building which faces the Ankara Palas Hotel across Cumhuriyet Boulevard.

"It is not," he said, "that we of the Arab League look with disfavor upon Turkey's alliance with the powers of the West. That almost certainly will come to pass. But it is no secret that there is still great and grave disunity within our organization [the Arab League], and that we have our malefactors—"

"The Mufti," I suggested.

Abdullah smiled quietly and went on. "Our malefactors— but we also have our statesmen and our warriors and great plans for the future peace and understanding of all the Arab peoples and their neighbors.

"This is not my first visit to Turkey," he said, "nor, I hope, will it be my last. Such hopes and aspirations as ours require long time for meditation and a firm meeting of the minds. The situation in Iran is very critical, but Iran is outside the framework of our League. Matters in Egypt will become very dangerous before summer is out, and Egypt *is* of the League, its very heart. I cannot speak for all our fellow members, but I know that every effort will be made to keep the peace in Egypt, in Syria [a reference to the Israeli dispute] and elsewhere. I shall do everything in my power to preserve it."

It is reasonable to suppose that King Abdullah *made* every effort. Only a few short weeks later, however, he was assassinated, and the Arab world lost one of the few great moderators in its slim fund of genuine statesmen. Abdullah's killer was a member of the *Jehad Mukabess*, a secret terrorist society controlled and directed from Cairo by the archvillain, the Haj Amin el Husseini, the former Grand Mufti of Jerusalem. Six other conspirators, including Colonel Abdullah el-Tel, former Governor of Jerusalem, were sentenced to death. The Colonel and a former Jerusalem vegetable merchant were sentenced *in absentia*. Four Arabs, including Moussa Abdullah el-Husseini, a cousin of the Mufti, were tried in Amman, sentenced to death and promptly executed in the first week of September.

Blood is as cheap as oil is plentiful, and murderous intrigue is rife in the sand-strewn Middle East. Behind the majority of the cold- and hot-blooded assassinations of Moslem leaders in the past six years in the Middle East lie the complots and intrigues of interlocking terrorist organizations. Behind the *Jehad Mukabess* (the Sanctuary of Struggle) terrorists lies the Moslem Brotherhood, and behind the Moslem Brotherhood and the semirespectable façade of the Arab League lie the cunning hand and the cold, fertile brain of the Grand Mufti of Jerusalem.

Before examining the extraordinary character of the Mufti himself, it might be well to recapitulate the thirteen assassinations which have rocked and swayed the embroiling Middle East since February 1945:

Ahmed Maher Pasha, Premier of Egypt, Feb. 24, 1945
Amin Osman Pasha, former Finance Minister of Egypt, Jan. 5, 1946
Mahmoud Fahmy Nokrashy Pasha, Egyptian Premier, Dec. 28, 1948
Sheikh El Banna, Egyptian Moslem leader, Feb. 12, 1949
Husni Zaim, Syrian President, Aug. 14, 1949
Muhsen Bey Berazi, Premier of Syria, Aug. 14, 1949

Abdul Hussein Hazhir, former Premier of Iran, Nov. 5, 1949
Lt. Col. Mohammed Nasser, Syrian Air Force Commander,
    Aug. 1, 1950
General Ali Razmara, Premier of Iran, March 7, 1951
Dr. Abdul Hamid Zanganeh, former Education Minister of
    Iran, March 25, 1951
King Abdullah of Hashemite Jordan, July 16, 1951
Riad el-Solh, former Premier of the Lebanon, July 20, 1951
Liaquat Ali Khan, Premier of Pakistan, Oct. 16, 1951

The Haj Amin el Husseini at fifty-nine is doubtless the
single most murderously dangerous man in the entire Middle
East. A master of deep intrigue and of incitement to blind
hatred and murder, he has sanctuary with King Farouk of
Egypt who, it is reported, is somewhat afraid of him. At any
rate the Mufti, a cautious little man and a professedly devout
disciple of the Prophet, carefully guards his health and his
vegetarian appetite, smokes not and drinks never. He takes
little or no exercise and has grown a trifle pudgy in consequence. His features, like his soft, well-manicured hands, are
delicate. His well-trimmed beard is gray. While on official
business the Mufti is attired in a full-length black robe and
a white turban. In his unofficial capacity, he wears the disguise
closest to hand—a business suit, a Bedouin burnoose or the
rags of a beggar.

Disguise is seldom necessary, however. As a descendant of
the Prophet Mohammed, Haj Amin is technically inviolate to
devout Arabs. When he travels abroad it is usually in state,
with a regal entourage, a bristling bodyguard and an advance
wave of intelligence agents to sniff out possible attempts upon
his charmed life.

Haj Amin el Husseini maintains his home and office in the Villa Aida, a pink and white establishment in Heliopolis in Cairo's suburbs, although he has ready access to Farouk's palace and to a spare office at the headquarters of the Arab League.

The Mufti is a busy man in his nefarious days and nights. Via radio and the official Egyptian news agency, palace tipsters and his own private intelligence service, the Haj Amin keeps his soft fingers ever upon the pulse of the entire world of Islam, the Occident and the Orient. Fabulously wealthy in his own right, the Mufti has only to command in order to draw unlimited funds from the strongboxes of the *Ikhwan el Muslemeen* (the Moslem Brotherhood), the *Jehad Mukabess*, or a baker's dozen of additional Arab secret organizations. The treasury of the Arab League is also at his disposal. The Haj Amin is personally guarded inside his villa by a picked crew of Palestinians who reputedly include the best pistol shots from among the Mufti's thousand-fold followers. Outside the villa, Egyptian police patrol between sentry boxes which ring the grounds. The grounds themselves are understood to be thoroughly wired and booby-trapped. The Haj Amin himself packs an American-made Smith & Wesson .38 police special, a snub-nosed deadly little weapon loaded with magnum high-velocity cartridges which will pierce armor plate. He tucks this inside his sash.

A snobbish intellectual, the Haj Amin is an omnivorous reader of all leading periodicals and books from everywhere in all languages. He speaks fluent English, French, German, Turkish and all Arab dialects, and has a smattering of Hindustani, Urdu and Japanese. The Mufti is a family man, with one wife and six children, including five daughters and a twenty-year-old son, Saleh. His personal retinue includes four male private secretaries and three chauffeurs who drive his armored limousines.

This writer was amused during a debate via radio and television in Washington this past winter to hear the Egyptian Ambassador, Mohamed Kamil Bey Abdul Rahim, haltingly assert that the Mufti is "in seclusion" in Cairo. The Mufti, on the contrary, makes frequent public appearances with or without King Farouk and the royal equipage, and was seated as the primary guest of honor during Farouk's annual Speech from the Throne last winter. The Haj Amin's public life is guardedly flamboyant.

It is his private life that concerns the worried West, for it is the avowed, burning, unquenchable aim of the Mufti to drive the infidel from all Islam and reign supreme as the religious and temporal leader of 50,000,000 Moslems.

The noisome activities of the Haj Amin during World War II are too well known for extensive recapitulation here. His pro-Axis activities in Jerusalem and his flight into Turkey; his solemn acceptance of Turkish asylum, followed by his flight (on the German courier plane) to Berlin; his violently anti-British broadcasts on the *Deutschlandsender,* and his escape to France following Germany's collapse are all a matter of record. His escape from Paris to Cairo and his renewed sanctuary with Farouk end that phase of his thumbnail history to 1948. In that year, the Haj Amin incited the *Ikhwan el Muslemeen* to overt acts against Israel. Out of them came the Israeli-Arab war. The Mufti persuaded Farouk to dispatch his Egyptian legions to do battle with the Israelis. The Egyptians were routed. Failing on the battlefront, which he had carefully avoided, the Haj set up the rump "All-Palestine" Government, with headquarters at Gaza and his nephew Jamal el Husseini as regent. It flopped, largely as a result of the Mufti's unrelenting feud with King Abdullah of Jordan.

Abdullah's steady ascendancy in power and prestige in the Moslem world infuriated the Haj. When Abdullah signed his separate peace with Israel and annexed Arab Palestine, he promptly deposed the Haj as Grand Mufti of Jerusalem. The Mufti threw caution to the winds and summoned the Moslem Brotherhood for a reign of terror. Something or somebody leaked, however, for Egypt's then pro-British premier, Nokrashy Pasha, outlawed the brotherhood and ordered a raid on the Villa Aida. Cairo police unearthed hidden arms stores, including some 3,500 rifles and more than 30,000 land mines, grenades and plastic explosives. Premier Nokrashy Pasha paid for the raid with his life. He was shot down by a Cairo medical student, a fanatical member of the *Muslemeen.*

The Haj dropped from sight, but only briefly. Early last year, he was off again. His first stop was Mecca, to renew his pilgrimage to the Moslem Holy City. "Haj," of course, means pilgrim. In his wake, as he flew eastward into Pakistan and Afghanistan, the Haj left a trail of verbal vitriol in violent speeches and closed sessions with underground terrorist leaders. In the wake of his visits came murder and naked connivance with Communism. Pakistan's army chief of staff, General Akbar Khan, was seized with a score of Communists as they planned the overthrow of the Pakistani government. Flying into Afghanistan, the Mufti rallied dissident leaders of the Afghan irredenta who are seeking to transfer some 7,000,-000 Pathan tribesmen to Afghanistan.

Border incidents sprang up. Even as Karachi began protesting to Kabul, the Haj was off again, this time into Iran. Ten years after he had tried to rouse the Iranian tribes against the British in 1941 (which led to the joint Anglo-Russian invasion of Iran), the Mufti popped up in Teheran to rouse the fanatical mullahs who already were plotting terrorism. The Haj Amin found plenty of comfort among the violent *Faydayan Islam* (Crusaders for Islam), one of the offshoots of the Moslem Brotherhood.

Warned to leave Iran, the Mufti traveled to Damascus. Even as he launched a vicious new anti-Israel campaign in Damascus and, later in the Lebanon, his spadework paid off in Iran. An assassin of the *Faydayan Islam* killed Premier General Ali Razmara, opening the way for the rise of Dr. Mohammed Mossadegh, who "nationalized" Iranian oil and precipitated the gravest crisis of the year in the Middle East.

Two of the Mufti's closest henchmen in the entire Middle East today are Abdurrahman Azzam Pasha, suave ex-Communist Secretary General of the Arab League, and pro-Communist Marouf Dawalibi who was premier for twenty-four hours in Syria last winter before Colonel Adib Shishakly called the Army and tossed him out.

The Haj Amin el Husseini is a ruthless renegade and a cold-blooded fanatic who will take every calculated risk to wreak havoc and bring the wildest disorder to the Arab world. If he brings it crashing down about his ears, "*Maleesh!*"— "So what?" The Haj, himself, will be in his bombproof shelter and shielded from the disorders by his formidable bodyguard. When the tumult and the shouting begin to die of the famine and pestilence and anarchy of revolution, then the Haj may be expected to emerge and seize the reins of power. The Haj, himself, may be riding a tiger of unsuspected voracity, however. With Communism in the saddle in the Middle East and the Mufti's real usefulness gone, the bearded head of the Mufti might well be the first to roll.

10

Truculent Egypt sprawls athwart the vital Suez approaches and the southeastern Mediterranean, somnolent, torpid, but dangerous as the sluggish vipers which haunt the tombs of the Pharaohs and the reeds and grasses on the Nile. From her desolate desert frontiers with Libya on the west, Egypt stretches along the Mediterranean littoral and across Port Said to the wedge of the Palestine Negeb, down the Israeli frontier and the Gulf of Akaba and the Red Sea to juncture with the Anglo-Egyptian Sudan in the Nubian desert. Vast in her expanse of 386,198 square miles, larger than Turkey and third in size among the Moslem states of Middle East —after Iran and Saudi Arabia—Egypt has a starveling, miserable population of some 20,050,000 *fellahin* who live in abject poverty and a figurative handful of landed wealthy aristocrats who encourage the most despotic monarchy in the whole of the Middle East.

Egypt's moneyed aristocracy, and King Farouk I, of course,

divide their time between their lavish town houses in Cairo and Alexandria and the French and Italian rivieras and European watering spots. The *fellahin* and their families swelter in hovels in the Cairo and Alexandria slums, in Port Said, Rosetta and Damietta on the Nile, at Suez at the southern entrance to the Canal and at Kosseir on the Red Sea. Ismailia controls the central span of the Canal and saw the bulk of the winter rioting which was checked by the reinforced British garrisons from Cyprus and the Sudan. The rest of Egypt's major cities and towns cluster along the fertile Nile delta.

Nearly all the foregoing is encyclopedic matter, however, and readily available in convenient trot form in any library. This chapter is concerned with history in the making in the turbulent Egypt of today and the chain reaction of dynamic events which threaten to force Egyptians into the forefront of the coming struggle for the riches of the Middle East.

The Egyptians neither have the stomach for the struggle, nor are they fully prepared for it, militarily or psychologically. The Arab has a childlike mind, although it is applied to worldly problems with deadly earnestness and fierce intensity. Egypt's protracted defiance of the West is based upon rankling years of misrule and British colonial and military arrogance, and what can only be described as bad timing.

The Egyptians knew, for instance, that Whitehall was preparing suggestions to modify the 1936 Anglo-Egyptian treaty at the very moment late last summer when Egyptian Premier Mustafa Nahas Pasha accepted a "mandate" from the people to abrogate it. The fact that the "mandate" came from howling, hashished street mobs organized and paid for, in large part, by the sinister Mufti and the Moslem Brotherhood and by Communist operatives—it is significant that two of the largest demonstrations were staged before the Soviet Embassy in

Cairo—was of little moment to Egypt's lawmakers. The fact that Premier Nahas Pasha, himself, had signed the treaty, which permitted the British to maintain garrisons in the Suez area to protect the Canal and in the Sudan, apparently mattered even less.

Mustafa Nahas Pasha, at seventy-six, has been battling British influence in Egypt through most of his kaleidoscopic political life. A member of the Egyptian Wafd (Nationalist) party since 1903, Nahas Pasha was alternately on the crest or in the trough of Egypt's stormy political squalls. Never very fond of King Fuad, Farouk's father, Nahas Pasha liked the young king even less upon his accession to the throne in 1936. The dislike and mistrust was mutual and rapidly ripened into downright contempt. Farouk abruptly tossed Nahas Pasha out of office in 1937 and in 1944, but the Wafd reinstalled him.

Once again, in January of 1952, Farouk tossed him out, but not until after the self-induced crises, during which the worried monarch and his distrustful first minister presented a common front to the British and Nahas Pasha had ramrodded a bill through the Parliament proclaiming Farouk the first King of the Sudan. The Sudanese were not consulted. As a matter of fact, reports from the vast Sudan, which extends some 1,650 miles southward from the Egyptian frontier to Uganda, covers nearly 970,000 square miles and contains more than eight million Sudanese, indicated that the Sudan wanted no part of King Farouk or his eighteen-year-old child bride, Narriman.

The British, still in technical possession, are holding out for free elections in the entire Sudan, when the Sudanese are deemed ripe for self-rule. Meantime, the Sudan has a legislative assembly, dominated by the Sudan Independence party. Spokesmen for the party sent word early in 1952 that the

Sudanese would reject any effort on the part of Egypt to impose the rule of Cairo.

In the troubled late winter of 1951–52, Cairo, Port Said and Ismailia still echoed to the occasional crumping of bombs, the rattle of rifle fire and the stutter of machine guns. The Haj Amin el Husseini, once more riding the tidal wave of popular favor with the fanatical Egyptian mobs, summoned the leader of the *Ikhwan Muslemeen,* Ahmed Hedeiby, and attempted to launch another terrorist campaign. Due to an unexplained shortage of arms and very real reluctance on the part of many Egyptians to travel down to Ismailia to be shot at, the campaign subsided rather abruptly. The Haj, however, chivvied Egypt's then Foreign Minister, Selah ed-Din Pasha, into a series of public appearances with him at which times both the speakers called upon the Egyptian government to sign a long-term pact of nonaggression with the Soviet Union.

True, such a pact had been hinted at by Moscow, but rumors are cheap in the Kremlin's propaganda mills, and a mythical agreement to keep the British off balance was real bargain counter material.

The Russians are too often underrated as students of racial psychology and social phenomena. For instance, it is a constant source of surprise to many Western minds that, to the Arabic mind, "the word is the deed"—the statement of a desired condition makes it fact. Arabs are notoriously in love with words and rolling phrases. Poetry and oratory are the language of the desert and the meat of the Koran, the bible of Islam. A study of the disparate Arab peoples over the years and over thousands of square miles in the Middle East discloses this phenomena again and again. Something said is something done: Allah has spoken, or been spoken to. The spoken deed is then totted up to history and, more often than not, that's the end of that. The Russians understand this sort of thing. Indeed, there is evidence to indicate that a kind of similar mysticism prevails among some Russians, where it has not been eradicated by the hard-boiled materialism of Red Army commissars.

The late Dick Sheepshanks of *Reuter's*—Sheepshanks was killed with Eddie Neil of the *Associated Press* and another British correspondent in 1938 in Franco Spain—was fond of relating an incident that points up this Arabic wish fulfillment. Sheepshanks and a small party of correspondents were waiting in a bitterly cold little *bodega* near Molina for a petrol truck to arrive with fuel for their exhausted motor convoy. Four Moorish troopers were huddled over a charcoal brazier in a corner while a fifth heated his stiff fingers over the coals and then strummed a guitar in a mournful *flamenco*. After a time, the petrol truck *did* arrive and Sheepshanks sent two of the Arabic Moors outside in the snow to tank up the convoy. Time passed. Sheepshanks grew impatient. He knew that a push was imminent on the Teruel salient. After forty minutes, Sheepshanks demanded how the gassing-up was going.

"Ah, it is done, oh, Master," said one of the Moors. The others nodded affirmatively. The correspondents gathered their gear and clumped out into the snow. The engine caught and hummed merrily. They had progressed perhaps half a kilometer when the lead car coughed, sputtered and ground to a halt. A second car was halted fifty yards back. Sheepshanks broke the blackout to flash his lamp on the fuel gauge. Empty. Furious, he turned on his Moorish aide.

The *Moro* shrugged. "*Inshallah!*" he murmured. "*If Allah is willing,* Master. We implored him."

It is a vast time-space transition, perhaps, between the approaches to the Teruel salient in another war in another country and some fifteen years ago, but there is a timelessness about the world of Islam and "modern" Egypt. Arabic philosophy has all the built-in modernity of the Gizeh pyramids.

Perhaps the most amazing and un-understandable phase of the entire Egyptian "shaky-do"—as the British Tommies call it—is the utter and obviously genuine indifference on the part of the Egyptians, and most Arabs, toward the titanic struggle between the democratic West and the Communist East. Insofar as the *fellahin* are concerned, this international conflict might well be a rather dull chess game or one of the obscure and strenuous games, such as cricket, that the Westerners persist in playing in the Cairo heat: "Mad dogs and Englishmen go out in the midday sun ..."

Even otherwise sound and reasonable Egyptian newspaper editors reflect some of this viewpoint. It extends even into governmental circles, although this correspondent found that, on higher levels, most Egyptian diplomats are perfectly aware of the perils inherent in steady Communist infiltration into the Middle East. Ironically enough, however, even the most intelligent and far-seeing Egyptian leaders are themselves victims of this all encompassing nationalism coalescing strange political bedfellows and cutting across hitherto unpassable party lines.

The strident Voice of America falls upon deaf ears and blank walls in most of the bazaars of the Levant where radios shriek and clamor at the top of their voices from dawn until the last thick coffee and the final fiery *arak* is downed long after nightfall. VOA's siren song of "democracy" and "free nations" is so much gibberish to most Arabs and nearly all Egyptians. The all-too-solid menace of engulfing Communism is not even a spectre or hobgoblin to the unhappy *fellahin*.

Stewart Alsop relates the story of an interview he wrote

with a Chinese Nationalist General in Shanghai in the spring of 1949. Shanghai in early '49 was still in Nationalist hands, as was most of China. Yet Alsop's Nationalist General blandly and quite cheerfully predicted that all China soon would be in Communist hands.

"Then," he said, with obvious relish, "you Americans will learn to take China seriously."

Westerners notoriously have experienced difficulties through downhill decades leading to the current debacle in China and the threatened disaster in the Middle East in taking the Asiatics seriously—or properly gauging the mettle and morale of the Moslem peoples.

To revert to Farouk briefly, for instance, the sorry spectacle of the Egyptian monarch lounging over the green baize gambling tables on the Riviera this past summer hardly was a picture to inspire confidence. The Anglo-Egyptian crisis grew from a tiny cloud on the Mediterranean horizon and swelled into ominous thunderheads before Farouk's nervous ministers could persuade him to look up from his roulette, poker and Gargantuan feasts.

"Farouk," a long-time British Egyptian resident told me, "had bloody well better cash in his chips and get back home and down to common-sense international politics, before it's too mucking late." Even the Egyptians themselves began to take a dim view of the King's extended yachting, swimming, gambling holiday with his child bride. Under official *ukase,* the Egyptian press abruptly ceased printing the colossal daily losses of Farouk at the gaming tables. It had been a point of pride for a while. Then it seems to have begun to occur to the Egyptians that the millions of francs and lire being raked in by the croupiers represented, after all, a sizable hunk of the national budget. Despite repeated warnings from Nahas

Pasha and Zaki Ali Oraby Pasha, the Senate president and a Wafd leader, Farouk repeatedly extended his stay in southern France and Italy. By the time he waddled back aboard the royal yacht with his holiday party, the crisis was full-blown.

Cairo for a time remained outwardly undisturbed, and there was not a ripple of unrest to disturb the tranquillity of the wealthy Greeks and Egyptians who swarm to the villas of Alexandria during the unbearable heat of the Cairo autumn.

The Cairo police, of course, are under strictest orders to canalize all demonstrations and rioting, unless the government itself orders a spontaneous "demonstration" where it will attract notice. Small wonder, then, that the incurious British and American diplomatic corps and thousands of travelers from abroad pooh-pooh'd dispatches in the foreign press reporting dangerous unrest in Egypt. (It was at this time that the Egyptian press censors began once more to scissor incoming copies of the *New York Times,* the European edition of the *New York Herald Tribune, Newsweek* and *Time.*) For instance, I had picked up just before my Istanbul-Beirut sailing an uncensored copy of a news magazine's "take-out" (full-length) story on King Farouk. This was the *only* uncensored copy aboard the American Export liner *Excalibur*—whose rather distinguished passenger list included Zaki Ali Oraby Pasha, the president of the Egyptian Senate, who had been attending the Inter-Parliamentary conference at Istanbul.

In these days of booming air travel, much useful ship lore probably has been completely lost upon globe-girdling businessmen, diplomats and journalists who know the nomenclature of airstrips, stratospheric weather and the far-flung routes of Pan-Am, KLM, TWA, Air France, BEA and BOAC. Such travelers miss the nonpareil camaraderie of the purser—an institution in ocean travel. The purser on shipboard is a

[94]

clearinghouse for all pertinent information: your banker, your go-between to the skipper, your tipster on the ship's pool, and a short cut to the attractive blonde on B-Deck or, in this case, an important Egyptian statesman.

Blackmail is an ugly word. However, I learned through Purser Cornelius Cronin that Zaki Ali Pasha wanted nothing so much as possession of my news magazine with the Farouk story. Through Connie Cronin, I sent word that it could be had for a price: an exclusive interview on the gathering crisis in Egypt. Shipboard gossip had it that the Egyptian Senate was about to take a special hand in the situation. The interview in Chapter Five was the payoff.

Jumping ship in Alexandria, I hired a car and raced up to Cairo to find—nothing. Nothing, that is, worthy of an immediate broadcast or cabled dispatches. On the surface, Cairo was the same old Cairo. Shepheard's, the Continental-Savoy and the sumptuous Gezirah Club hummed comfortably with subdued conversation over tall drinks and, after teatime, equally subdued music from behind the potted palms. A swing around the city revealed little more. The filthy back streets and the corners off the boulevards still swarmed with diseased beggars, prostitutes and pimps, "gully-gully" boys— magicians of a low order who also specialize in pocket-picking—and the usual pushcarts laden with fly-covered fruit and cheap gewgaws for the tourist trade. The shimmering heat, the dust and an occasional gust of wind carried the same raucous braying of donkeys and the foul odors of the sewers, camel dung and unwashed bodies.

Footing it back in later from Zamalek, the residential section which houses most of the foreign diplomatic corps and Cairo's wealthier families—cocktail stopovers which elicited nothing more than local chitchat, "business as usual" and, of course, cocktails—I tried very hard to come at the real, challenging wrongness of the whole picture. A taxi turned up at the Nile and, en route back to Shepheard's, more of the picture slipped into focus. The fundamental characteristic of Egypt, like most of its Middle Eastern neighbors, is that it is a way station, just a port of call en route somewhere.

This rising tide of nationalism, so unapparent on an Egyptian Sunday, workaday to the Egyptians and a holiday to the foreigners, was, inevitably, going to continue to climb. But is nationalism a policy? Without any firm economic foundation and without any social bulwark for the miserable Egyptians—totally without effective defense—Egyptian and Moslem nationalism constitutes a glaring weakness and a grave danger. Nothing startlingly new here, certainly, but every face of danger is different, even in the Middle East.

Shepheard's. In the bar, the usual quota of professional ladies. Summing up my notes on a busy day and evening, it seemed there *was* a dispatch here if I could get down to it. Over a second gin sling, as frequently happens, the idea looked even better.

Egypt and the Levant way stations no longer. At long, desperate last most of the West, including the Americans, were beginning to take the Middle East dead seriously.

But were they—*are* they? My friends in Zamalek attested no such turnabout. Unhappily, too, most of the 40,000,000 Arabs in the Middle East still seem disinclined to come to any firm understanding with the West. Egypt had indicated already that she would spurn any suggestion of a five-power command over the Suez Canal, for fear of domination, still, by the United States, Britain, France and Turkey. Genuine internationalization, then? Would Egypt welcome, for instance, a Soviet gunboat or submarine flotilla off Suez or in the Red Sea? More importantly, would the West tolerate such action? Would the Turks torpedo a fundamental tenet of their foreign policy and permit genuine internationalization of the Straits of the Dardanelles? To all these questions, a probable *no*.

Collective security is the primary problem—with the proposed Middle East Defense Command a step along the way, another way station in the formation of policy.

Nine of the ten potential members of the Middle East Command were and are still virtually indefensible against any major attack from Russia. Turkey alone is prepared instantly to defend herself and work in coordination with the Southern European Command and the Strategic Air Command which would be delegated to plant the big bombs in the Russian interior. Under proper conditions, Greece could maintain a kind of temporary holding action. As for Syria and the Lebanon, Israel, Jordan, Iraq, Iran, Egypt and Saudi Arabia, the indifference and torpor of the Levant overlie them like the deadly dusty heat of the enervating *khamsin,* the south wind that sucks away courage as one sleeps.

11

SPRINGTIME IS MEANINGLESS to some three and a half million fierce Bedouin tribesmen who roam the vast deserts and pitch their tawny tents in desert oases or near the scattered sun-baked cities in the 1,100,000 square miles of Saudi Arabia. Only the blowing of the springtime *khamsin*, the parching "fifty-day wind" from the south, and the ungainly amatory antics of their camels and scrawny, hard-bitten sheep tell the nomadic tribesmen when the winter is gone and the voice of the theoretical turtle (dove) should be heard in the land. With one possible, recent and highly newsworthy exception—the thunderous roar of giant airplane engines in this uneasy spring, as the United States Strategic Air Command exercises its prerogative to beef up the mighty Dhahran airdrome, making it the most formidable Western air base in the entire Moslem world.

A theoretical theocracy, Saudi Arabia is an absolute monarchy under an iron-handed septuagenarian, Ibn Saud, who takes a million dollars plus per year from oil royalties and in exchange maintains a limited Open Door policy toward the United States and the West.

The one barred door to all infidels in Saudi Arabia is the gate to the Holy City of Mecca, the shrine of Islam, the birthplace of Mohammed. Elsewhere, in theory, Americans—particularly oil engineers and surveyors, airmen and anthropologists—are free to roam at will. King Ibn Saud's 15,000-man army, with motorized and mechanized units, a maneuverable camel corps and speedy Arab irregulars, ride herd on all foreigners and marauding renegade tribesmen who still forage over the frontiers from the wilds of Iraq.

King Ibn Saud himself is a giant of a man, almost seven feet tall and still vigorous in his seventy-second year, although he is nearly blind in his right eye and his hearing is impaired. While he has a fleet of specially built Rolls Royces and Cadillacs, *lagniappe*, in most cases from the British and the Americans, and private airliners, Ibn Saud can still outride most of his entourage—atop a camel or astride one of his prize Arabian stallions—and outtalk tough Texas oilmen on leases, drilling rights and royalties. A hard-boiled, self-made monarch, Saudi Arabia's big king is implacably anti-Communist and, in these treacherous days in the Middle East, a good man to have around. The Americans and the British are carefully bending their efforts to this end.

The Saudi Arabian peninsula is a giant trapezium, counting some 1,400 miles from Aden to Akaba, now a Jordanian port on the strategic Gulf of Akaba leading into the Red Sea, a port which Ibn Saud has long had an acquisitive eye on; some 1,250 miles from Aden to Ras Al Hadd on the lower Persian Gulf; and roughly 900 miles to Fao which, in turn, lies 750 miles east of Akaba. Encompassed in this endless area are

[99]

wilds and wastelands as desolate as the dreariest of all Iraq—old Mesopotamia—a handful of Arab cities including the capital, Riyadh, Medina and Mecca, villages along the ancient routes of the camel caravans and oases with trickling springs and welcome palms. From a narrow coastal plain along the Red Sea, steep mountains rise from 5,000 to 10,000 feet (near the southern end of the peninsula) and bulwark the vast plateau which slopes gently eastward toward the Persian Gulf.

While the torch of Islam burns brightly throughout North Africa and all but a minuscule few thousand square miles of the Middle East, it blazes nowhere more fiercely than in Ibn Saud's desert kingdom. Ibn Saud consolidated his realm upon the bedrock of the Moslem faith and a system of centrifugal tribal relationships and loyalties, and lashed it all firmly together through the creation of agricultural colonies. He was still in his twenties when he turned from desert campaigning to weld his subjects into unity, first in the central and southern Nejd, which with the Hejaz formed the kingdom of Saudi Arabia. Because Saudi Arabia, Kuweit, Bahrein and the Trucial sheikhdoms of Oman and Mukalla upon the Gulf of Oman loom so largely in the current world-wide struggle for oil, the entire peninsula and its monarch must be subjected to something more than passing attention.

Ibn Saud Aziz ibn Abdurrahman ibn Feisal was born in Riyadh itself in 1880. He was the son of Abdurrahman, who had been the youngest of four sons of the Emir Feisal, who ruled as Sultan of the Nejd from 1834 to 1867. Fleeing the Nejd with his father during the 1891 invasion by Amir Muhammad, young Ibn fetched up in Kuweit where he was taken under the wing of the Sheikh Mubarak ibn Sawah, a lordly Arabic leader who had come to terms with the British in their first infiltrations around the Persian Gulf and the Gulf of Oman.

Young Ibn learned much more than statesmanship from Sheikh Mubarak. He learned desert lore and warfare and intrigue. At the turn of the century he was ready to attempt recapture of the lands from which his father had been driven.

Ibn set forth northwestward in the desert with less than 200 picked men. In a genuine commando raid, Ibn picked fifteen of his most ruthless followers and invaded Riyadh after nightfall. The raid was successful. He slew the local governor of Ibn Rashid and mounted the throne of the Nejd. In the next fourteen crowded years, King Ibn Saud drove the Turks from the Arabian peninsula and so impressed the British that they treated the young monarch with the utmost deference, risking his anger only once. The British backed Hussein, the father of Abdullah of Hashemite Jordan, in the struggle for the Hejaz. Ibn surprised and wiped out the Hashemites at Turaba. The British then retreated to diplomacy and in the Kuweit Conference for six long months sought to persuade King Ibn to cease and desist. Triumphantly, Ibn Saud launched a tremendous campaign which carried everything and everybody before it. By 1926 his forces had occupied Mecca, Jedda and Medina. He was undisputed king of all he surveyed.

And what he surveyed was considerable. Gone forever were the fat and indolent, greedy and grafting Turkish Emirs who had milked the Nejd and Hejaz of wines, women and taxes. Gone, too, were the raiding Rashidis who had plagued and marauded outlying oases and villages along the Iraqi frontiers. King Ibn added motor transport and modern weapons to his cavalry and camel corps. From his own crude version of a modern agricultural administration, with headquarters at Artawiya, Saud saw his farming colonies grow to more than a hundred throughout the Nejd.

Anglo-Arabian relations flowered like Ibn's desert. The

desert king mended his political fences as he fended for his people. A vigorous man, Ibn Saud probably has had more than one hundred and fifty wives, although it is considered rather bad form to discuss his domestic affairs. He had, at last count, some thirty-five sons whom he has brought up in the best traditions of Islamic creed and Arabic philosophy, British schooling and a finishing course with the hard-riding camel corps. His eldest son and heir apparent to the throne of Saudi Arabia is Ibn Abdul Aziz Saud, viceroy of the Nejd—although another son, Emir Feisal, holds the foreign ministry portfolio and reigns as viceroy of the Hejaz during Ibn's frequent trips into the interior and his rare journeys abroad.

Amid the warlike rumblings in the oil-soaked Middle East today, Ibn Saud's kingdom is a model of peace, propriety and prosperity in the best Islamic tradition, with certain modern improvements. The big Arab king will have no truck with Communism or the agents of the Soviet who have been infiltrating every Middle Eastern state since well before the end of World War II. Known Communist *agents provocateurs* are tabbed at the frontier and carefully watched. The recent influx during the last winter of scores of Soviet *commerçants* was rigidly controlled. Culpable agents are warned, whereafter their visas are canceled and they are escorted over the frontier. Second offenders simply disappear and, bazaar gossip has it, are put to the sword in the best Arabic tradition.

King Ibn Saud rules his nomadic subjects and the well-paid oil workers with a stern but highly benevolent hand. He supervises his vast dynasty with an intense interest in the personal welfare of its people and an eagle eye, his good one, to his mounting oil royalties from the rich deposits in Saudi Arabia.

Californian Arabian Standard Oil Company, a strictly American concern, made the first major deal with Ibn Saud in

1933. Since then, the king has never looked back, financially. Saudi Arabia's wells pump up the bottomless oil sea at a rate of better than 600,000 barrels per day, the second largest production in the entire Middle East and the fifth largest in the world.

Aramco runs the works; this, the Arabian-American Oil Company, is a 30-30-30-10 venture divided, respectively, among Standard of New Jersey, Standard of California, the Texas Company and Socony-Vacuum. A humming refinery at Ras Tanura on the Persian Gulf pumps out nearly 200,000 barrels per day for the tankers which queue up in the blinding, soaking heat of this waterway. The famous Tapline, a 31-inch pipe line, was completed last year and now funnels 300,000 barrels of crude oil per day across the trackless wastes of Arabia to Sidon on the Mediterranean.

The oil industry is not only one of the most vital in the world; it is one of the toughest, most demanding trades and professions devised by man to bedevil himself. And there are only a few other areas in the world, most of them near-by, in which the hours, the labor and the nervous stresses and strains are less than in Saudi Arabia. The engineers and drillers and riggers and laboratory technicians who operate Aramco's vast holdings in Saudi Arabia are the best that the profession has produced and that money can buy. The women who follow the men must be made of stern, if malleable, stuff. Limited air-conditioning against the blinding, searing heat and PX (post exchange) privileges—whiskey, gin, cigarettes, cosmetics, canned goods—lighten the burden somewhat. But it is a deadly, grueling existence for man and woman alike, and for the children. Inevitably there are crack-ups. Like the sere and ramified life on an army post, the lives of Dhahran's growing colony of American expatriates are regimented by the

[103]

heat, working hours, weird Middle Eastern *tabus,* and by the colonists themselves. Dhahran is subtropical and the *khamsin* blows, and if otherwise normal Americans succumb to atmospherics and behave at times like characters out of Somerset Maugham, *Maleesh!* Nobody, insofar as this writer could ascertain, has yet begun to maintain actuarials on Americans in Saudi Arabia—although company books would indicate the risks and rates on probable alcoholics, hypochondriacs, nymphomaniacs and other sex athletes who turn up in odd, out-of-the-way places under certain conditions, usually surprising themselves more than they startle their fellow colonists.

Like the notorious *kona* weather of Hawaii, the *khamsin* takes a murderous toll of its Western victims in all the Middle East, including Saudi Arabia. Not even the natives are proof against it. Stabbings, suicides, sex crimes shoot upward. And in the foreign colony, the rather dumpy little Kansas-born wife of a rigger begins to look especially attractive to a lanky, introverted engineer from East Texas, with consequent fireworks.

Perhaps it is a tribute to the rugged constitutions of these far-flung American oil pioneers that the crack-ups are steadily diminishing in number. Or the screenings are getting tougher, at the Stateside end, according to some new arrivals. Whatever the reasons, the end result is that Americans are becoming firmly entrenched in one of the furthermost outposts of the endless Middle East behind the pillars of defense erected so solidly by Ibn Saud.

Not that the enemies of the West are not chipping away at the defensive barriers erected by Ibn Saud and immensely strengthened by the growing American colony in Saudi Arabia and the giant base at Dhahran. Via Rome and from Beirut, the unofficial Communist party headquarters in Middle East,

Communist agents and the renegade operatives of the Grand Mufti of Jerusalem from Cairo are infiltrating Ibn's desert kingdom in ever-larger numbers. Not even Iran has seen more sedulous and concentrated underground operations by the common enemy. But, whereas Iran was spread for months under the glare of news dispatches and the unending communiqués issued during the Anglo-Iranian crisis, Saudi Arabia has been largely neglected as a source of "hard" news.

"Hard" news—as opposed to any other *genre* of news—is a term invented by and for the use of harried, frustrated editors of press associations, newspapers and, particularly, radio networks, who are firmly convinced that the public can digest only news that is firmly capsulated and can be swallowed painlessly without any harmful effects upon the patient. The more distant the essential news and the harder to come at—with ensuing overhead in travel and communications—the "softer" the news becomes, in the view of the editor and the auditing department, and, besides, it could tend to obfuscate the radio commercial or distract the reader from the advertising matter. This is true of Middle Eastern news in general. The distances are immense and communications uncertain, and in particular in Saudi Arabia travel is outrageously expensive and radio and telegraphic communications are almost nonexistent. And it is doubly true of Middle Eastern developments which have lain like a ticking time bomb under Western diplomatic and military missions and installations through these last few crucial months and years.

Saudi Arabia is of course a member of the Arab League. The spiritual heart of Araby and all Islam lies in Saudi Arabia, at Mecca. The very nature of the League itself, however, impels its central headquarters to a permanent location in Cairo. Ibn Saud's personal power and integrity dwarf the Arab

League's leaders and call forth invidious comparison with their brazen opportunism in embracing Communist dogma, thinly disguised, and in the use of Communist funds, arms and *agit-prop* in the attempted undermining of order everywhere in the Levant. The political posturings of the Haj Amin el Husseini and Abdurrahman Azzam Pasha, the League's secretary general, have not been lost upon the Arabic peoples of Saudi Arabia. The king himself has given the League and its incessant intrigues and confusions as wide a berth as possible—and even offered his services as mediator of Anglo-Egyptian disputes.

From the stark and sandy desert wastelands of his vast kingdom on the Arabian plateau, Ibn Saud surveys the vital microcosm of the entire Middle East with an air that has been defined by his few intimates as sternly paternalistic. Lest this be interpreted as lese majesty, his Arab chieftains recall that King Ibn, like Mustapha Kemal of Turkey, put his own house in order, gently but firmly wherever possible and with ruthless force when he felt it necessary. Like Ataturk, King Ibn Saud took the robes of benevolent dictatorship and, like the great Turk, has worn them well. The Arab monarch's relations with the West are as circumspectly even as only a proud ruler's can be, and as coolly correct as a cash register. If he is occasionally and seemingly disdainful or even contemptuous of Arab rantings in the bazaars of Damascus and Beirut, Amman or Cairo, he seems to temper his regard with understanding—that the fervor of Islam needs the cooling benison of common sense. As for the Russians, Ibn Saud looks upon them narrowly as a hybrid of pariah dog and pit viper—hungry, treacherous, cunning and mordant.

12

M ILES AND MILES of Sweet Fanny Adams, the modern independent Arab Kingdom of Iraq—old Mesopotamia sliced off the Ottoman Empire—boasts some 4,799,000 subjects, 116,600 square miles of desolate desert, and one of the richest oil lodes in the world. (Sweet Fanny Adams is a euphemism of old Middle Eastern hands for a rougher phrase meaning miles and miles of virtual nothingness.) Iraq is a theoretical constitutional monarchy headed by seventeen-year-old King Feisal II who takes his orders from Regent-Premier Nuri as-Said, sixty-four, who dominates the Iraqi senate and lower house and in turn is gently dominated by British Middle Eastern policy.

A militant member of the Arab League, Iraq is feverish with the heated nationalism infecting all Islam and prey to Communist infiltrations from neighboring Syria and Iran. Her three and one-half divisions are rated good desert fighting men, but the army's British equipment is old and outdated and its air strength is worse than negligible. What makes Iraq so desperately important to the British and the West?

The answer is oil from the rich Basrah, Mosul and Kirkuk fields—and new deposits discovered near the Syrian-Turkish frontiers—pipe lines, and Iraq's strategic position near the heartland of the sweltering, rumbling Middle East. Iraq is bordered on the southeast by the incredibly oil-rich sheikhdom of Kuweit and the Iraqi outlet to the Persian Gulf via Basrah and the Shatt-al-Arab river; on the south by the long, trackless frontier with Saudi Arabia; on the southwest by Hashemite Jordan; on the west by Syria; on the north by Turkey; on the north and northeast by Iran. More than two-thirds of Iraq's predominantly Moslem peoples live in wretched poverty along the ancient Tigris and Euphrates rivers and amid the filth and squalor of her major cities, the capital, Baghdad, Mosul and Basrah. Iraq, too, is a periodic victim of the enervating *khamsin,* but the predominant wind is the *shamal* which blows, sometimes with fierce, gusty intensity, out of the northwest. Dust storms are commonplace, for the erosion of centuries has left the vast plains and uplands helpless before the *shamal* which tears at the ruins of ancient Babylon and filthy, modern Baghdad as it did in the first century A.D. Perhaps nowhere in all the Middle East is irrigation more desperately needed, with the moneys and the planning to make it possible, and almost nowhere else in the Arab states could so much be done with so little.

Oil may be the answer. Poor in minerals, Iraq is turning at long last from agriculture, spinning and weaving and the grim life of nomadic shepherds to the ancient oil springs which flowed richly even in the time of ancient kings.

Cut off from Haifa's tanker fleets by the Israelis, in consequence of the Arab-Israeli hostilities, the Iraqis now pump their oil in stepped-up quantities from the Kirkuk and Mosul fields to Tripoli on the Lebanese Mediterranean shore and to Basrah on the deep, crocodile-infested Shatt-al-Arab in the south. The hopeful new oil strikes in northwestern Iraq, northeastern Syria and southeastern Turkey, with relatively short distances to deep-water ports or to the growing pipe-line web, may enrich these areas beyond all current calculations. Oil royalties then could pay for irrigation projects, farm implements and modern agricultural methods which could make the desert bloom as it bloomed four thousand years before Christ.

Any writer on the subject of the Middle East has a constant struggle with himself, and most of us are perennial losers. The temptation to drench the reader in the romance of history is almost overpowering. Archaeologists and anthropologists writing of Mesopotamia are doomed from the outset. Carlton Coon's otherwise excellent book *Caravan* is a case in point. It is interesting from the anthropological point of view to trace the fortunes of the country from the times of the Hittites, the Assyrians, the Persian conquerors (including mighty Cyrus), the period of Hellenic pomp and glory, the Parthians, the Sassanian period and down to the Arab conquest of ancient Iraq (southern Mesopotamia) and Jazirah (northern Mesopotamia). It was the hardy Turks who delivered the *coup de grâce* to the peoples of old Mesopotamia. Tough as the Arabs, but trained and disciplined, they rode roughshod over the courageous but divided tribal leaders in the Jazirah and Iraq. Like the ruthless *foederati* of the Teutonic legions which sacked Rome, the Turks swarmed down to pillage Baghdad and turn Iraq into a wilderness. Hulagu Khan, the son of Genghis Khan, launched a campaign of conquest unprecedented in the history of the times. Iraq became a wasteland of swamps and steppes. Embankments were destroyed and canals drained. The farmers were slaughtered or driven into temporary sanctuary in the villages and towns. The Turks and the Persians fought fiercely over prostrate Iraq until Suleiman the Magnificent stormed Baghdad in 1534 and overran Basrah twelve years later.

From the sixteenth century to mid-way in the twentieth there seems to Westerners to be a gaping chasm. In the timeless Middle East it is virtually two ticks of the clock. But the historical chasm can and must be bridged if one is to come at the essential reasons behind the emergence of modern Iraq as a keystone state in the Middle East and a vital Western beachhead in the conflicts of the immediate future.

War, characteristically World War I, first directed Western attention to the incalculable possibilities in Mesopotamia. Turkish corruption and cruelty had already set the stage for Arab risings. When World War I exploded in Serbia in the nearby Balkans, it was but a step to the catatonic confusions which rent and split the tribes of Mesopotamia—and then loosely united them for the backdoor conquest of the Turks through the Middle East.

The Anglo-Indian campaign and the Allenby campaign in Palestine were linked with the clandestine desert warfare of the fabulous Lawrence of Arabia. Allenby's operations, better reported, and Lawrence's exploits—half legend, half truth—captured the headlines and the public imagination of the day. The foot-slogging campaign of the hard-driven Sixth and Twelfth British Indian divisions in "Old Mess-pot" were largely ignored. With the arrival of the Seventh and Third British Indian divisions from the Western Front in Europe, the British offensive in Mesopotamia began really to move. Kut fell after Baghdad, and the Turks, outnumbered four to one, gave up Kirkuk in bloody fighting. Mosul followed, and the British Indian Army was regrouping for a massive offensive when the armistice came on the Western front. The triumphant Arabs vastly overrated their contributions to the downfall of the Ottoman Turks—but the British cagily kept them in line. From a British mandate, Iraq became a kingdom under Feisal I in 1921 and in 1932 reached full-fledged independence.

The woes of independence are multitudinous, as the Iraqis discovered. Unready and unfit for statehood, the Arab leaders found and still find themselves beset by vast problems, political, economic and military, far beyond their comprehension. Into the inevitable power vacuum vacated by the Ottoman Turks, the British moved with all the finesse and *sahib* psychology nurtured in their Indian colonial adventures. British responsibility for Iraq's defense and security was a mandate of World War I. The hard-pressed British regard that mandate as still completely operable today and they are determined to exercise it.

Wisely at first, and then out of necessity, British ground troops were withdrawn and Iraq's defense was consigned to the air force and to Iraqi divisions, armed and trained by British officers. The British diplomatic mission to Baghdad was re-enforced by the best brains Whitehall could muster. Unfortunately, many of the best brains available had been honed and stropped in the British Colonial Office to cut through colonial problems in the manner of Victorian High Commissioners, viceroys and proconsuls. Consequently, as in Iran, Egypt and elsewhere in the Middle East, the British found themselves almost as hated and detested in Iraq in 1939 as the Ottoman Turks had been feared and despised in 1914.

By the skin of their teeth, the British held the Middle East with their traditional "two men and a boy," through the dreadful and darkling years of 1940–43. This writer has no intention of recapitulating the kaleidoscopic history of World War II in the Middle East, aside from occasional jogs to the memory of a highly forgetful Western world which had had its fickle attention directed elsewhere for the most part. It is unmistakably a fact that almost no one who was not in the Middle East at the time of the fall of France fully could appreciate the calamitous effect of French surrender upon the French Army of the Levant in Syria; of the splintering of the French Army and the effect of that splintering upon the embattled Turks, already committed through the Pact of Ankara to alliance with the Allies, and the near-catastrophic events in Iraq which followed straightway.

With the possible exceptions of Egypt and Syria, no other Middle Eastern power could change more swiftly for better or worse, with more dire consequences upon Western political and military fortunes, than the Kingdom of Iraq. Historical parallels are tricky, yet Middle Eastern history is rife with examples of stratagems and treacheries, sellouts and complots, subtle intrigues and gutter cunning unrivaled before or since Machiavelli. It is no good, moreover, to expect American diplomacy and our shallow fund of genuine, worldly diplomats to anticipate and cope with Islamic mysticism, Arabic philosophies and Levantine connivings which have set even the hardened, experienced British by their ears.

Iraq is a case in point. The British themselves were caught awesomely short in Iraq in 1940. France had fallen and with its collapse contradictory orders were flashed to the French Army of the Middle East. Faraway France in surrender controlled the destinies, via the striking forces of the French

Army of the Levant, of Turkey, the slim British garrisons of the Western Desert and Iraq and the still hodgepodge British Second Indian Army which had been alerted to move, too late, from India to the Middle East.

Official France, in surrender at Compiègne, ordered the French Army of the Levant to lay down its collective arms. Frenchmen abroad, including governmental and military exiles who had fled to sanctuary ahead of the *Wehrmacht,* dispatched orders that the French Army was to fight on. The French Army of the Levant was a rough, tough, hard-bitten organization which included unregenerate scoundrels drawn from the ranks of the Foreign Legion, Germans, Balts, Poles, Jews, Belgians, Russians, Turks and others, French-officered.

The fate of the Middle East, almost literally, hung by a hair. Had the French Army in Syria followed the German *Diktat* from Paris, Syria would have fallen overnight to the enemy; Turkey, isolated, would then have been confronted with the ultimatum the Wilhelmstrasse never quite mustered courage to deliver—*Axis membership or invasion;* the exorcised Arabs of Jordan and Palestine already were on the brink of a rising, under the aegis of the Mufti and Rashid Ali el Gaylani and their notorious henchman, Fawzi el Kaukji. *And Iraq?*

The German enemy, like the Communists today, had laid their plans well and deep. That these plans miscarried is more a tribute to Rashid Ali's abortive attempted *coup d'état* in Baghdad, general Arab confusion and garbled reports from Beirut and Damascus—contradictory intelligence regarding the ultimate decision of the French Army leaders—than to British or American prescience. Indeed, even as the Iraqi artillerymen rolled up their field guns to fire on the American Embassy compound at Baghdad, the American mission still clung to the belief that it was all a weird dream compounded

[113]

of the prevailing confusion. Under no such happy delusion, the British belatedly manned the gun ports with side arms and prepared to sell their lives dearly. The German plans, hatched in Turkey, had envisioned no such walkover, and when German reconnaissance planes were ordered to Baghdad to establish a Middle Eastern Axis basis, the Wilhelmstrasse suspected a trick.

By the time the first ME-109's actually had landed in Baghdad to find the airdrome in the hands of pro-Axis Iraqis, reaction was setting in. Churchill had ordered General Henry Maitland Wilson to mount his extraordinary offensive, in cooperation with the disorganized but patriotic Free French remnants of the French Levantine Army, and march upon Damascus. It mattered very little that General Wilson's forces were minuscule, under-armed and desperately short of ammunition. In the eyes of the Arabs, the word was the deed. Churchill's desperate audacity and General Wilson's miserable little column of Bren-carriers with a handful of British troops and a spattering of Free French *did* march, and ultimately take Damascus. "Jumbo" Wilson, as he was irreverently known throughout the Middle East, was only one prong of a two-pronged attack—according to a news broadcaster working out of Ankara at the time. This young man was sold one of the howlers of that year and all time in the Middle East by the British military attaché in Ankara.

According to the story peddled by the British, a powerful, hitherto unheard-of British motorized force of considerable proportions had somehow materialized near Aleppo in Syria and was proceeding by forced marches upon northern Iraq along a line roughly paralleling the Syrian-Turkish frontier. Dutifully, the young American broadcaster reported nightly to his network upon the progress of this ghost column. It was readily apparent to all concerned that no such column existed or ever had existed, but it had been created and the American newscaster kept it moving—rather in the manner of Evelyn Waugh's flamboyant war-correspondent hero in his pre-World War II book *Scoop*. That character, it will be recalled, barricaded himself in his hotel room with a typewriter upon his lap, a map on the wall and a handful of darts on the bed-side table. Each morning this worthy would blindfold himself, hurl a dart at the map and where it landed was the date line for the day. The correspondent got wonderful cables of congratulation from the home office.

Rather like Waugh's intrepid correspondent, the American broadcaster in Turkey moved his phantom motorized column across the wastes of northern Syria toward the Iraqi border. The broadcaster was becoming desperate and his New York headquarters were reflecting decided impatience with the slow-moving column of mysterious relief troops when a handful of British and loyal Iraqis put down the Baghdad rebellion. The ghost column was conveniently forgotten. It still lives, however, in the legends of old Middle East hands; charitably it never has been printed, for the broadcaster is in business today in Washington, for another network.

Such comedy relief is rare in the Middle East today. Communists are notoriously humorless where the stakes are high and the chips are down. The Haj Amin el Husseini and his renegade associates in Iraq and elsewhere have evinced no humor whatsoever aside from the sardonic self-assurance that, using any means and any allies, they mean to hurl the Westerners out of Iraq and the entire Middle East.

British operatives of the Iraq Petroleum Company are quite adamant about their position. The Iranian oil adventure has taught them a thing or two. In Iraq, with certain advantages including the presence of the British military and air force, they have brought off a new ten-year contract governing pipe lines, the Alwand refinery, and royalties from the major Iraqi oil fields at Khanaquin, Basrah, Mosul and Kirkuk. Iraqi engineers, according to terms of the new agreement, will take over the Alwand plant and oil-distribution facilities presently controlled by the Khanaquin and Rafidain Oil Companies which are subsidiaries of the Anglo-Iranian Oil Company. Such oil as they produce, however, will be for internal consumption.

American, British, French and Dutch interests are all concerned with Iraqi oil, but the British stubbornly have let it be known that over-all policy will be controlled from London. Barring some unforeseen and totally outside development, this would seem to be the *status quo* for the beclouded future as envisioned by all concerned, including the Iraqis. Soviet policy, and that of the Mufti, in Iraq, have not been disclosed.

13

THE TORCH OF ISLAM blazes fiercely in the mountains and deserts and swamplands and *wadis* of Arabic Syria where some 3,300,000 chauvinistic peoples guard 66,046 square miles of strategic terrain, suspiciously eyeing their neighbors on all frontiers. From legendary Damascus, the oldest continuously populated city in the world, descendants of ancient kings and slaves feel keenly the low political barometric pressure which threatens storm in the unruly Levant and perhaps still another engulfment by tides of empire from without.

Crossroads, battleground, melting pot and a charnel house through bloody centuries of conquest, modern Syria is a curious political experiment which even the lowliest Arab beggar in the bazaars senses is still in a state of evolution. Of all the troubled states in the Middle East, it could be said most truly of Syria that she has been Balkanized, again and again, and like the Balkans, the very atmosphere of Syria carries the effluvia of intrigues and treacheries.

As in the explosive Balkans, too, Syria has been a cat's-paw of French and British colonialism and the iron whims of their administrators. The Syrian peoples themselves are curiously, almost rigidly, divided between peasants and nomads and wealthier townspeople, and they mingle only in the common fealty to Allah and Mohammed. The Druses of the Djebel Druze dwell in their heights in something like contemptuous isolation from the Damascenes and the tobacco planters of Latakia, and the desert tribesmen of the northeast share mutual fear and distrust with merchants and craftsmen of Aleppo and Homs.

Syria's Djebel Druze and its basalt heights rise along the Hashemite Jordan frontier in the south. Westward lies the disputed and dangerous wedge of frontier with the hated Israelis. Due west is the Lebanon republic, split off from Syria in 1941, now prosperous, cultured, half Christian and somewhat disdainful of the mother country. The eastern Mediterranean littoral is Syria's western border northward to the Sanjak of Alexandretta, wrested from Syria by the Turks in 1939—some 1,900 square miles of historic ruins, malarial lowlands and tobacco fields—now called the Turkish Hatay, derived from its Hittite background. Due north, of course, lies the long west-east frontier with powerful Turkey. While the Turks have evinced no interest in expansionism since they annexed the Hatay, the suspicious Syrians regard Ankara with narrowed eyes.

Turkey is strong politically and sound economically, despite the fearsome drain on her treasury by a standing army of 27 divisions, and the Turks have only begun to exploit the long-suspected mineral wealth beneath the soil of the barren plateaus which extend southward to the Syrian frontier from the Taurus mountains. No, the Syrians presently have no quarrel with the Turks, nor the Turks with Syria. But a latent element for conflict recently has been discovered in drillings beneath the high, barren, volcanic Harran Plateau on the Turko-Syrian border: oil.

Oil engineers are plumbing this high Mesopotamian area today seeking final proof of oil deposits which may dwarf even the immense oil seas which flow beneath Saudi Arabia, Iran and the petroleum-rich sheikhdoms of the Persian Gulf. Round and about Urfa in southeastern Turkey just north of the Syrian border, French geologists have discovered chains of "mud volcanoes" which experts attest are positive proof of giant oil deposits. In one sector, the geologists mapped 145 such mounds, varying between 150 and 900 feet in circumference and extending over an area more than 22 miles wide and 70 miles long.

A lean, powerful and well-armed Turkey with the incalculable riches of a giant oil field, refineries, railroads, pipe lines and nearby waterways, including Iskenderun (Alexandretta) in the Turkish Hatay, is a spectre which haunts the dreams and waking hours of Syria's political leaders. The Western world may have forgotten the colossus of the Ottoman Empire which bestrode the vast reaches of Western Asia, the Balkans and southeastern Europe, but the peoples of these areas have not forgotten. Nor are they likely to.

Looking due eastward, the anxious Syrians focus on Iraq and their one fairly reliable Arab neighbor in the event of a general Middle Eastern conflict. While the Hashemite Jordan dynasty is regarded in Damascus as weak, corrupt and probably doomed to early trouble, Iraq—with British bolstering—is held a potential ally and perhaps an ultimate member of a

[119]

Greater Syria to include Syria, Iraq, Hashemite Jordan and nearly 1,000,000 miserable but fanatical displaced Palestinian Arabs. This dream of a genuine Arabic confederation went glimmering with the murder of King Abdullah of Hashemite Jordan, but it could be revived, according to some Syrian statesmen. The Arab superstate has a ready-made king, seventeen-year-old Feisal II of Iraq, who is nearing his majority when he can take over from the Iraqi regency.

Such Arab dreams, of course, are the stuff of nightmares to the Israelis who protested vociferously last winter against reports of an Iraq-Jordanian merger and the transfer of British troops to the neutralized Gaza strip bordering the Egyptian Sinai and Israel. Intrigue is second nature to the Syrians, and, while there may be nothing more to the rumored rebirth of the Greater Syria plan than the rumors themselves, the Syrians may be expected to keep them humming and buzzing in the ears of the despised Israelis.

One major barrier that would have to be surmounted in any case is sheer Syrian nationalism. Arab nationalism was not born yesterday or yesteryear (although it required the Iranian and Anglo-Egyptian crises to bring it to the attention of the inattentive Western world). The spark of Syrian independence was kindled and fanned into flame in 1908 by the Turkish revolution itself. Increasing contacts with Western civilization already had spurred a degree of cultural renaissance and a modernization of Arab poetry, art and written history. Nationalist agitation continued to grow and flourish through World War I, and the Arab revolt in Syria in 1916, while it was crushed bloodily and ruthlessly by the Turks, was to rise anew.

Feisal I undertook to insure his peoples' postwar independence by waging a fierce campaign against the Turks in Trans-

Jordan and Mesopotamia. Feisal's legions drove to Damascus as Lord Allenby waged his victorious Palestinian campaign and the British Indian armies mopped up at Kut, Mosul and Kirkuk. The war ended.

Perfidy then supervened in the shape of arrogant French colonialism. Despite Anglo-French joint declarations, only four days before the 1918 armistice, that Syria and Mesopotamia would be granted self-government, the French suddenly demanded a mandate over Syria. The Arabs protested, then revolted. Desert warfare followed and the French smashed Feisal's armies, entered Damascus and sent Feisal into exile. The British, contributing their share to this Middle East model of divide-and-rule, boosted Feisal onto the Iraqi throne and ousted Abdullah to Trans-Jordan.

Syrian violence continued. Revolts flared outward from Damascus, from the Djebel Druze and Tripoli. The French then hit upon the happy idea (to them) of a quasi-independent state of Lebanon. The Christian population of the mountainous sectors of the Lebanon speedily agreed. Syria was then split, or Balkanized, into four so-called states, allegedly autonomous—the states of Damascus, Aleppo, the Djebel Druze and the state of the Alawis with its capital in Latakia.

The inflammable Druses exploded first. The Sultan Pasha el Atrashi struck in July 1925, marching on Damascus where nationalists from Latakia and Aleppo and the Damascenes joined the Druses in what became a full-blown revolution. One of Syria's great patriots, Dr. Abdur Rahman Shahbandar, established a revolutionary government in the hilly fastnesses of the Djebel Druze. The French shipped more troops from Marseilles and transshipped bloodthirsty units of the Foreign Legion from the Rif. The French besieged Damascus and in a two-day bombardment blasted the ancient city, destroying some of its priceless and historic public buildings. Paris then rushed Henri de Jouvenel to Syria to negotiate a settlement. The Syrians received a treaty, but it was a weasel-worded document which left the French ample room for continued domination. Unrest continued.

Italy's Ethiopian adventure and the consequent tension in the Mediterranean forced both the British and the French to come to terms with the Islamic peoples of Egypt and Syria. The Iraqis already had secured their nominal independence. Under the muzzle of a general strike, the stubborn French at length invited a Syrian mission to Paris to sign a more liberal Franco-Syrian pact. It still held out for French air bases on Syrian soil, for the supplying of French arms exclusively to Syrian troops, and for armed French garrisons in Latakia and in the Djebel Druze. At the same time, the French "negotiated" a treaty with their puppet Lebanese regime and secured the right to maintain armed forces in the Lebanon as well. The haughty French were sowing the same dragon's teeth that the British had planted earlier in the Levant.

World War II set the stage for the French collapse in the Middle East and unleashed the pent-up furies of the down-trodden Arabic Syrians. General Maxime Weygand was yanked away from his Syrian command over the French Army of the Levant in the desperate, futile effort to rally the French armies on the Western front. With France's fall, Weygand's successor in Syria, General Eugene Mittelhauser, announced that the French Army in Syria would obey the pro-German Vichy government. The German and Italian governments dispatched armistice commissions to Syria, allegedly to supervise demobilization, actually to transform French bases into Axis centers for operations against the British in the Middle East. Axis agents, paid by Reichsambassador Franz von Papen from his headquarters in Ankara and the elaborate German spy ring operating from Istanbul, filtered into Syria in alarming numbers.

The notorious Rashid Ali el Gaylani already had launched his revolt in Iraq and proclaimed himself premier. Arab leaders in Syria and elsewhere in the Middle East witnessed the smashing German victories in the Balkans, the fall of Greece and the collapse of Crete, and concluded that the Axis had victory in the bag.

It was touch and go for long, nerve-wracking weeks. Fresh from the disastrous Balkan campaign and the collapse of Yugoslavia, this writer sped to the Turko-Syrian frontier to cover the Arab revolt, German aerial operations and the beginnings of British resistance. Gallantly and audaciously, the British stripped precious units from the British Eighth Army and rushed them via Palestine into Syria and toward Iraq. Spread desperately thin throughout the Middle East, the British forces nevertheless spear-headed the Free French battle in Syria against the Vichy forces of occupation.

The British at the same time did a masterful diplomatic job with the Arabs, particularly in Syria. Britain firmly disavowed any political or territorial aspirations in Syria or the Lebanon. Credits were offered and the depression-ridden Levantine states were hooked onto the British wartime economy and the sterling bloc. It was one more severe strain on the already dwindling British financial resources, but the British preferred losing pounds sterling to precious manpower which was in extremely short supply. Under severe pressure from Whitehall, Washington recognized the serious situation in Syria and dispatched George Wadsworth, a veteran career diplomat, to Beirut as diplomatic agent and consul general.

As the advent of World War II had unloosed potentially

cyclonic forces of revolt in the Arab world, the close of the war and eleventh-hour Anglo-American diplomacy, coupled with quick economic assistance and genuine planning and construction, brought order out of chaos and aroused hopes for a genuine *rapprochement* between vital portions of the Arab world and the West. With British help, the Syrians built rail lines between Beirut and Tripoli and from Beirut to Haifa, opening through rail travel from Turkey to Egypt and to Iraq. The outlook was splendid for a while.

As bankrupt statesmanship at top levels torpedoed Allied military victories almost everywhere, however, so did the immediate postwar blunders wreak havoc with the promising beginnings of bona fide Western influence and power in the Middle East.

The scrapping of the United States army, air force and still essential war production and the mothballing of the fleet were no less disastrous than the complete letdown of all Western effort in the Middle East. In almost a twinkling the British and the Americans pulled their installations and their ablest administrators out of the Arab world, and yanked the props from under the building economies of Syria and the Lebanon, Iran, Iraq, Jordan and Egypt. Forty million Arabs who had only begun to taste the sweetness of limited independence and a sufficiency of food suddenly were reduced to their prewar dunghill existence. The militant Israelis, meantime, burning with an unquenchable desire for statehood, backed by apparently limitless funds from abroad and inflamed by the unspeakable atrocities of the German death camps, chose this moment to strike their blow for Israel.

The Arab-Israeli struggle has been touched on in earlier writing and will be examined anew, for the issues are deep-laid, persistent and dangerous. In present-day Syria, the status of Israel, Palestine and the Arab refugees looms horrifyingly large to these deeply emotional and fanatical peoples. It has become inextricably entangled with the violently knotted skeins of Islamic revolt, Arab nationalism, xenophobia, dynastic conflicts, and the unremitting struggle among the great powers for the precious oil and for waterways, ports, bases, power and influence in all the Middle East.

Syria lies athwart the modern routes of empire in the Middle East as surely as her peoples guarded and sometimes pillaged the camel caravans of antiquity which crisscrossed her bloody sands between the Greco-Roman empires and the dominions of the east. Syria could not escape her geographical fate, even if her peoples wished to. Syria is committed to a key role, perhaps a dominant part, in the dramatis personae of the swiftly unfolding tragedy in the Levant. Tied politically to the venal and corrupt Arab League and still fettered economically to ruinously outmoded methods of agricultural production and transport, Syria and her peoples live culturally in the dim past, victims of the enervating hashish of Islam and the wishful word-deed philosophy of Araby.

Syria is nonetheless dangerous. As this is written, Syria is ruled by Colonel Adib Shishakly, a wiry, fatalistic but hard-driving military dictator who seized power late in 1949. Shishakly can muster 25,000 courageous but ill-trained troops, underarmed, with one armored brigade of outdated French equipment. Syria could raise perhaps 100,000 desert warriors in a prolonged emergency, but without arms or equipment. Damascus and Aleppo have their quota of Communist agents and reliable information indicates that the Mufti's following is considerable, probably in the neighborhood of 55,000 faithful. Communist orders and agents could be pumped into Syria within a matter of hours from the Middle Eastern Communist headquarters in nearby Beirut. And Moslem Communists from the Soviet have been filtering for years into Syria via Iran, Iraq and the desolate wasteland country of the northeast.

From nearby Cyprus the British watch Syria and the Lebanon with hawklike attention. The storm signals, when they are hoisted, may well fly first at this strategic corner of the eastern Mediterranean.

14

COMMUNIST PENETRATION of the Middle East is deeper, deadlier and extensively more tenacious than ever has been accurately reported or reflected in the random newspaper dispatches, broadcasts and editorialized essays haphazardly relayed by visiting correspondents who touch down in Ankara, Beirut, Damascus, Teheran, Baghdad, Riyadh, Amman, Tel Aviv and Cairo, and wing on. The author freely admits past guilt on this score, culpability ranging backward to the closing years of World War II, and with the additional, damning admission that the hard facts were there all the time. Extenuating circumstances, in the light of history, are negligible.

The plain truth is that Communist agents have infiltrated every nationalist movement within the Middle East and that the appalling inroads made by the Russians have gone unreported, for the most part, by otherwise able and reliable foreign correspondents, or have been buried on the back pages of American newspapers or junked as insufficiently news-worthy by the editors of press associations, newspapers and radio networks.

Censorship, indifference abroad, the pressure of deadlines and arrant stupidity have teamed up with tireless Communist propaganda and subversive elements within the American and British governments to blind the Western peoples to the real Soviet aims in the invaluable Middle East. As China went, so goes the Levant, and with it are going the oil, the bases, the ports and waterways, the road- and railheads of 2,000,000 vital square miles, some 40,000,000 Moslem peoples, one and a half million Israelis and some half million Christian peoples of the Lebanon.

Lebanon. Here is a tiny republic, a reluctant Arab League member, in its eleventh year of independence, with a population of 1,228,000 and a minuscule army of some 6,500 loyal but underequipped troops. Here is the center, in Beirut, of the entire Middle Eastern ring of Communist espionage, pay-rolls, sabotage and terror, political murder and international intrigue extending from Pakistan and India through the Levant to the furthermost reaches of the Islamic peoples in northwest Africa.

Communism injected from the Lebanon is not the stock model exported to other quarters of the world. It comes in a score of guises, variously ticketed, but usually labeled nation-alism. It is hideously effective. Let there be no mistake about this. Soviet propaganda incessantly preaches by radio in a dozen languages and dialects the fable that Arabic peoples are constitutionally unsuited to Communism, as Communist *agit-prop* successfully sold the story that Chinese Communists were merely "agrarian reformists." Illiteracy and political ignorance are no barrier to Communist inroads in the Middle

[128]

East. Blaring radios in the bazaars and Communist, Arabic-speaking agents cover the Middle East like the relentless desert sun which bakes its deserts and mountains.

It is ironic but desperately true that wealthy, intellectual Beirut and the relatively well-to-do Lebanon should be the poisonous center of Communism in the Middle East. Relatively without a history of their own, the inhabitants of the Lebanon nevertheless have played extraordinary roles, since the time of the Phoenicians, with the campaigns of conquerors in the Mediterranean and western Asia since 3,000 years before the birth of Christ. Biblical history treats the Lebanese as merchandisers in timber, grain and olive oil deals between Hiram of Tyre and Solomon of Israel. The Lebanese displayed a special dexterity in rolling with the punch of history, and of emerging virtually unscathed from the invasions which scourged the kingdoms, later the sheikhdoms, about them. Even Turkish rule was relatively benevolent. Lacking the surly spark of revolt, the Lebanese knuckled under, paid their taxes and satisfied the fat Turkish emirs who ruled until the explosive Arabs rose to join the Allies in the desert campaigns which overthrew the Ottoman Empire. Characteristically, the Lebanese were useful putty to the French who used them to insulate the French mandate over Syria and ride out the gathering storm of Arab revolt in the Levant in the years following World War I.

The little Lebanon encompasses less than 3,700 square miles, but Beirut, the capital, is the pleasantest and perhaps most modern city in the Middle East. Imported French culture lingers on. So does commerce. The fallen French were expelled from the Lebanon, but French capital and business acumen still mesh in velvet-smooth commercial operations which have been the despair of designing Britishers and American upstarts who remain baffled by the centuries-old cunning of the Levantines.

Shipping contracts mysteriously slip away. Silk, tobacco, olive oil, myriad fruits and long staple cotton flow out of Beirut and Tripoli in unending streams, and the shippers are Lebanese, masked, sometimes, with converted French capital. Sidon gushes 300,000 barrels of oil per diem into waiting tankers at the quays, crude which has been piped more than 1,000 miles from the Aramco drillings in Saudi Arabia. Lebanese royalties are fat and growing fatter. New oil strikes in northern Syria and southeastern Turkey may be expected to find their first egress from Middle East via the Sidon pipe line.

Lebanon and the Lebanese have riches to burn, and the shrewd business heads to preserve their wealth. The Lebanese are disdainful, but not toplofty, toward their Arab neighbors about them. They manage to maintain a graceful equilibrium under the most trying political circumstances. Financially secure and intellectually dominant over their Middle Eastern neighbors, the wealthy Lebanese forcibly remind one of England's late Cliveden Set, pre-Hitler; of the Polish prewar aristocracy; of the lovable but weak and vain Jan Masaryk of Czechoslovakia, and, inevitably, of the lunatic fringe of American "liberals" who so idiotically espoused or adopted the Soviet policy line in the darkling years of 1942–43–44–45 and early '46.

Perplexed Middle Eastern observers, provided they stick around that long, usually come to the sixty-four-dollar question: *Why do the Lebanese tolerate Communism?* The Communist party is outlawed in most of the Middle East, although Communist front parties are tolerated in Egypt, Iran and, occasionally, in Jordan.

Candidly, the Lebanese seem to take a kind of perverse

pride in Moscow's abiding interest in Beirut and the Lebanon. The Russian operatives, Moslem-born and Arabic-speaking and thoroughly trained in the Moscow East school, keep their political noses absolutely spotless while on the job in the Lebanon. Their incomes are fabulous, in comparison with Communist operatives elsewhere, and the life in the Lebanon is paradise. The Hotels Normandy and St. George are excellent, as are smaller hotels and pensions, and Beirut cuisine is French-Arab-Armenian and superb. Women are plentiful, beautiful and amiable. Communications are excellent. There is brilliant sunshine and cobalt water for swimming in the milder spring, summer and autumn months and magnificent skiing in winter. One can motor from the dry heat of Beirut to the breathless loveliness of the great hills which overlook the town in half an hour.

And obviously the Communist operatives have no immediate interest in the Lebanon *per se*. The Lebanese Sûreté, French-trained, has yet to uncover a single positive scintilla of evidence that Moscow directly threatens Lebanese security. The suave minions of the Lebanon's tourism offices beam on all travelers arriving via *Air France, Pan-American World Airways,* Egypt's *Misr Airlines* and spur services, as well as the hundreds of tourists who troop ashore from the cruise ships which daily dot Beirut's swarming harbor.

Lebanese complacency toward Communism would seem to have diverse explanations. One excellent reason is that the payoff is good. Russia is funneling enormous quantities of gold into the Lebanon and it finds its way into the private coffers of governmental deputies and appointees.

The large Russian colony in Beirut and the Communist operatives at Tripoli, Sidon and Tyre are free-spenders and they meticulously behave themselves. Russians who do misbehave are yanked unceremoniously from the Lebanese flesh-pots forever. The Russians never meddle directly in Lebanese internal affairs—which, unhappily, Anglo-American opera-tives often do. Then, *baksheesh* is expected, and readily forth-coming from the Russians, for special governmental favors. Neither the State Department nor the U. S. Army and Navy maintains a slush fund for approachable foreigners.

The late, lamented Riad el-Solh, independent Lebanon's first Prime Minister, was a thoroughgoing but lovable scoun-drel who was shot to death last July just four days after the Mufti's assassins in Jerusalem murdered King Abdullah of Hashemite Jordan. The fact that Riad Bey was out of office at the time supported the Lebanese official explanation that his killers were embittered members of his waterfront gangs who had been deprived of their cut on a lucrative looting expedition on the wharves. The cold fact that Riad Bey was a genuine Lebanese patriot and an enemy of the Mufti was pointedly ignored. Riad's waterfront connections *were* incon-testable. But Riad also was militantly anti-Communist and vigorously opposed to the inflammatory tactics of the Mufti. Plus the fact that Riad was one of Lebanon's really able leaders among its small revolving fund of politicos and sooner or later would have been in high office again.

Lebanese foreign policy is not, like Egypt's and Iran's, being made in the streets. It swings like a compass needle from pole to pole, East to West, to the points of greater strength, but the political polarity is carefully surveyed and nudged gently in the proper direction by the Lebanese quidnuncs themselves.

Lebanon is comparatively wealthy and reasonably stable, then, politically, even in the worsening atmosphere of the uneasy Arab world. Beirut remains a major money mart for the entire Middle East. The Tripoli and Sidon pipe-line outlets bolster Lebanese economy, and, of course, financial Beirut still controls some 50 per cent of Syria's trade and exerts strong influence on Iraqi and Jordanian commerce. A new refinery is being constructed at Sidon to absorb some of the burden of crude oil shipped from Aramco's fields in Saudi Arabia. This project, like the Litani river hydroelectric and irrigation program, is American-inspired and -financed. Syria's cotton boom, especially, has given a lift to Lebanese economy and every incoming freighter in Beirut harbor bears its quota of cotton-ginning equipment, cultivators, tractors and pumps for Syria's new Euphrates irrigation projects, all more grist to the Lebanese mill of commerce.

On the surface the picture is dimly encouraging. Actually, it is deeply misleading. As in Syria, the richer Lebanese are growing richer and the poor, poorer. The small farmer's heritage of free land is vanishing, drying up in irrigation projects which ultimately may work wonders for the thirsty desert but which do little in the critical interim for land-hungry peoples. Lebanese wages are severely depressed by overpopulation and by the burden of nearly 100,000 Palestinian refugees.

Statehood has engendered very little patriotism in the breasts of young Lebanese, especially the women. This is one possible explanation for the tenacious grip of Communism on the Lebanese youth. The bogus "nationalism" being sold by Communist agents in all the Arab states is a by-product of Moslem anarchism carefully distilled by the Russian makers to the individual taste. As stressed earlier, it is largely for export from the Lebanon, but a certain amount inevitably is siphoned off for local consumption. The growing effect is perhaps not precisely what the Communist operatives intended but, adaptive as they are, the Communists are utilizing

Lebanese emigration abroad, especially to the United States, with considerable effect.

Immigration visas for Lebanese bound for the United States are highly restricted. Under the present quota system there is a wait of five years or more. There is, however, no quota on "students." All that is required is a letter from an American college or university and boat or plane fare. And the Lebanese colonies in the United States are extensive and still growing. The marriage trade, Stateside, for young Lebanese women is flourishing. The marriages usually are contracted in Canada, whereafter the Lebanese brides or bridegrooms return to the United States to become American citizens. A very considerable number of them conduct extensive correspondence thereafter with relatives and associates in the Lebanon and money is exchanged. One recent estimate indicated that nine out of ten Lebanese "students" who emigrated to the United States remained there, either as brides or bridegrooms or, conveniently, as forgotten aliens, making excellent field workers for the international Communist party. Lebanese passports are notoriously easy to come by, almost as cheap and procurable as Central and South American citizenship credentials during World War II.

There is, possibly, a certain amount of cool comfort in recent assurances from American immigration authorities that this trafficking in citizenship is under study, and that the status of thousands of Lebanese presently in America will be subject to re-examination. No one is more politically and emotionally concerned, perhaps, about this issue than Charles Malik of Lebanon. A genuine patriot with a solid knowledge of the West, Malik has been a tower of strength in the United Nations where he functions as the chief delegate of the Lebanese mission. Like Selim Sarper of Turkey, Malik has been a

[134]

powerful voice of conscience speaking from the heart of the troubled Middle East, as deeply stirring and disturbing to the other Malik—Yakov of the U. S. S. R.—as to such political changelings as Sir Benegal Rau of India, Ales Bebler of Yugoslavia, the confused litany of Arab League spokesmen and the highly polished but ambiguous Acheson and Philip Jessup of the United States.

Charles Malik is gravely disturbed about the internal affairs of his country, but he is vastly more troubled by the seething problems of the explosive Middle East. Too long ignored, these problems are hideously distended today like some cancerous tumor which threatens to burst and send its deadly poison coursing through the system of the whole area. Malik, again like Sarper of Turkey, recognizes that the solution to the Middle Eastern dilemma goes beyond the military lancet and the economic swab; that law, religion, culture, philosophy and a whole way of life are concerned, but Malik, like the handful of real statesmen grappling with this dreadful issue, also knows that time almost literally has run out.

There is no substitute for armed forces in the Middle East today. There is no substitute for the economic aid which must bolster the tottering regimes of Iran, Egypt and Jordan, rotten as they are, lest they collapse under the flood tide of fanaticism and open the way for Communist supremacy. Turkey could possibly stand as a lonely, craggy promontory, but the vassal Balkan states and Greece and Iran, Iraq, Syria and the Lebanon, Israel and Jordan, Saudi Arabia and the Persian Gulf sheikhdoms and Egypt would go down like ninepins before any determined Soviet assault. Pakistan and India, on the eastern periphery, have neither the will to withstand nor the matériel to repel aggression from the Soviets. Libya, Tunisia, Algeria and Morocco on the western periphery of the Middle

East are nakedly vulnerable. The Balkan approaches, again, are wide open and a Communist Yugoslavia cannot be counted upon to support a Communist dictator, Tito, in mortal combat against overwhelming legions of the Russians who installed Tito in the first place.

The tiny and virtually defenseless Lebanon is a fitting observation post from which to survey the Middle East. That the survey, as sighted by this writer, is predominantly military is, regrettably, unavoidable. Western resistance to naked Soviet aggression has been reduced to the irreducible minimum of what military men call "hardware"—at present guided missiles, atomic and biological warfare, jet-propelled aircraft, Schnorkel submarines, vessels of the fleets, and, of course, the flesh and blood of manpower trained to the tanks and the guns and the small arms necessary to storm and occupy the terrain without which victory still is impossible.

It is still almost axiomatic that men of good, or pretended, good will never abandon the fiction of diplomatic make-do— even though the logical extensor of all diplomacy, force of arms, has received its order of battle. That the order of battle has not yet been clearly drawn in the inevitable Middle Eastern battleground is directly traceable to thoughtlessness, superficiality and arrant stupidity upon the highest levels of the planners in Washington and London and, of course, to the ruinous and bankrupt foreign policies which, consecutively, have undermined Anglo-American relations with the Moslem world, state by state, nation by nation, people by people.

In the preceding portions of this work, the author has sought to examine at first hand the enormously complex problems which have brought the Western world to its present impasse in the Middle East. Groundwork has been laid for the reporting and analysis to follow. No study of the Middle East makes sense without an examination of its vast but integral periphery, the nearby Balkans, Pakistan and India, waterways and canals and ports, harbor installations, North Africa and the Mediterranean itself, and—within the increasingly narrow framework of security—the measures under way for the war which the United States and its allies must fight in the near future in the bloody, oily sands of the endless Middle East.

15

THE MORAL CHALLENGE of the Middle East is stupefying. Were Soviet Russia and her terrorized satellites to disappear tonight in some improbable celestial clash of the political spheres, the challenge would remain. It would be less fraught with appalling immediacy, but remain it would.

Iran and Egypt are embarked upon fanatically nationalistic policies which can lead only to national suicide, or worse. Hashemite Jordan, in the inflammable center of the Arab world, shows every sign of following suit. Restive Iraq is a tossup, especially if Haj Amin el Husseini and his Communist allies coalesce in a complot to explode a *jehad* or Holy War in the Arab states. Syrian stability hangs by the tenuous thread of a single life, Lieutenant Colonel Adib Shishakly, who has been lucky thus far. Israel is a weird, artificial microcosm existing on the intoxicating flames of racism and newborn nationalism which would be snuffed out in a twinkling without financial oxygen from the United States. Israel, moreover, is literally between the devils of ravening Arab hatred and dis-possession and the deep blue of the eastern Mediterranean. No one who has not explored the Middle East can fully under-stand the blind, unreasoning, murderous hatred which exists between Jew and Arab—nor appreciate the bitter irony of the fact that Anglo-American political policies are largely respon-sible for it.

Aside from Israel, oil is the wealth and the curse of the Middle East. Ibn Saud of Saudi Arabia and the sheikhs of Kuweit, Bahrein, Qatar and Trucial Oman are waxing fat on incredibly rich oil production. New drillings in Turkey and northeastern Syria promise what geologists and oil engineers have believed for almost a century, that Turkish and Syrian fields may dwarf even the rich, paraffin-laden crude of Iran and her now-fallow fields and the gigantic Abadan refinery. This oil beckons the oil-thirsty Soviets as well as the West. Iranian fanaticism, Mossadegh and sedulous work by the Com-munist Iranian Tudeh party temporarily have deprived the British and the West of Iranian oil production, a signal victory politically, but no thoughtful Middle Eastern observer be-lieves that the stubborn British and rugged Americans can long be restrained, short of war, from exploiting the riches of the Iranian, Iraqi and potential Turkish and Syrian fields.

Short of war: here is the Middle Eastern challenge, flat out. The moral qualities are implicit, for they have been spelled out in recent years by the Arabian-American Oil Company in higher wages, improved working conditions, shorter hours, hospitalization, pensions and wealth, comparative wealth, to Arabs who lived before upon the levels of their animals, sheep, goats, camels, donkeys and dogs. The British Anglo-Iranian Oil Company ignored and even derided American personnel policy, while expanding the Abadan refinery to make it the greatest in the world and meanwhile operating with a colonial policy that dated back to Victorian times.

When the roof fell in on British colonialism in the Middle East, there was premature laughter followed by a few cries of "shame!" (especially from U. S. Ambassador Henry F. Grady in Iran)—cries emanating from the American improvisers of foreign policy in the Arab world. W. Averell Harriman was rushed to Teheran at the insistence of Dean Acheson upon a mission that can only be compared with Nevile Henderson's to Hitler or Joseph Davies' to Moscow.

The irremediable damage had been done, years before, in dereliction of diplomatic duty and presently in a kind of wringing-of-the-hands before the catastrophe of Iran. Grady's recall was too late, and Loy Henderson's appointment too tardy, to right the wrongs that had gone before. Mossadegh's flying visit to the United States, and his extended conversations with George C. McGhee, Assistant Secretary of State, got precisely nowhere.

The Egyptian debacle followed. Rudderless, the Wafd Party which controls the wayward Egyptian government was beset by the storm of nationalism sweeping the Middle East. Premier Nahas Pasha frantically radioed King Farouk of Egypt at the gaming tables on the Italian and French Riviera. Nahas Pasha, who is not too fond of Farouk, anyway, received no instructions, and gave leeway to Selah ed-Din Pasha, the former Foreign Minister, who is known among his Middle Eastern colleagues as—the word is funny in the Middle East, but would be interpreted as libelous in the West.

The rest is bitter Egyptian history. Nahas Pasha had been warned repeatedly that the British would take no nonsense over the Suez Canal and the status of the Anglo-Egyptian Sudan. Washington mumbled, but Admiral Carney spelled out for Selah ed-Din Pasha the firm intent of the U. S. Sixth Fleet to go the limit in backing the British in the defense of Suez. Eisenhower, it might be added, authorized the Carney paraphrase. This overshot Eisenhower's technical authority, but time was short. Moscow also had seized this moment to attempt the exertion of new pressure upon Turkey—during the course of the Inter-Parliamentary Conference at Istanbul, including the old chestnuts about Soviet claims to the provinces of Kars and Ardahan and Russia's earlier avowed interest in the "policing" of the Dardanelles.

Foreign Minister Fuad Koprulu of Turkey did not even consult President Celal Bayar of Turkey on the radioed messages from Istanbul, the site of the Inter-Parliamentary Conference. He gave the Russians a flat, unequivocal rejection of their note within half an hour. It might be added that the U. S. Ambassador, George Wadsworth, was advised of the context of both notes.

It might also be added here that the entire Arab League, with the Lebanon a reluctant dissenter, had sought to exert pressure upon the Turks to give some kind of lip service to Iran and Egypt. The Turks strove through all diplomatic channels to heal these breaches but refused absolutely to back the Iranian stand on the ouster of the British or to underwrite any policy move which would endanger the stability of the extremely queasy eastern Mediterranean.

It would seem to be politically and ethnically, even militarily, logical to switch here from the Middle Eastern states to their bordering Asiatic neighbors. Pakistan, India and Nepal, with Afghanistan, would seem to be, pragmatically, the next logical theatre. Yet to a correspondent trained on Balkan wars and intrigues, and with the special variety of Soviet Communist infiltration in this area, the dynamic, unpredictable Balkans overshadow the Middle East today in a pattern that cries out for coverage.

First of all, of course, is the dynamism. Communist domination has no more quenched the fires of Serbian nationalism, doused Bulgarian irredenta nor smothered the flames of Hungarian patriotism than the heel of any tyrant could reach the heights to stifle the wild goat cry of the cliff-dwelling Albanians. The Ottoman Turks overran the Balkans and stormed the gates of Vienna, but they could not eradicate the fire of the Serbs, nor put down the murderous hatred of the Macedonians.

The spark plug of the Balkans is Yugoslavia, a misnamed and vastly misunderstood country of magnificent peoples who are a whole world in miniature. Misnamed, because Yugoslavia was artificially created out of the geographical rubble of World War I, lumping the indomitable Serbs, the wily and toplofty Croats and the lovable Alpini Slovenes with the conglomerate mixture of Dalmatians, Hercegovinans, Bosniacs, Macedonians, Montenegrins, Greeks, Bulgars, Turks and ragtag and bobtail of peoples who fetched up in this mountain and forest kingdom from the steppes of Asia, the warm shores of the Adriatic and the Aegean and the grim fastnesses of the black mountains which rise like spectres from the mists of Montenegro.

Yugoslavia today is riddled with tyranny and further diseased with the bloody, feudal chancres of hatred between Serb and Croat, Croat and Serb. Our Western challenge in the Middle East is enormous, but our problem in Yugoslavia is perhaps greater. Because in Yugoslavia the United States and Great Britain sold out a man and a people, for reasons of cold-blooded, shortsighted, downright stupid political and military expediency—a policy which will cost the West dear.

The people of the Balkans have long memories. Fabled in song and story, the heroes of the Balkans never die. This is especially true of the Serbs. Warriors, poets, schoolmasters, the tall, rugged Serbian peoples, peasants and artisans conserved some inner fire which defied conquerors from any compass point.

Such a man was Draja Mihailovich. In the tradition of the Serbs, Draja—"Chicha" or uncle, as we knew him—rose from a colonelcy at Mostar to lead the Serbian Chetniks, guerrilla irregulars, against the Axis enemy throughout World War II. Forsaken by everybody, including his king, young Peter II of Yugoslavia, Mihailovich desperately fought on against the common enemy—the back-stabbing Hungarians, the traduced Bulgars, the miserable Italians and the despised Germans— and killed more than the plague. He ordered his men to build an airfield and from that strip rescued more than 700 Allied airmen, Americans, Britons, Aussies, New Zealanders, South Africans, who left their woolly uniforms behind for their protectors and who can testify today to Mihailovich's undying hatred of the Axis enemy.

Mihailovich is dead, foully murdered after a drumhead "trial" by the minions of Josip Broz ("Tito"), the Communist dictator foisted on postwar Yugoslavia by the Russians. The body of Draja Mihailovich was so riddled by tommygun fire that it was unrecognizable in the cellars of Belgrade prison, and then the remnants were tossed into an unmarked grave to avoid an honorable burial. The State Department, the Communist-infiltrated OSS and the OWI aided the Tito Government in suppressing the exonerating evidence; evidence which never was needed by the Allied fliers who were on combat missions against the Axis enemy with General Draja Mihailovich during the period when it was heinously alleged that this

[143]

gallant Serbian leader had—in the weasel words of Winston Churchill, since retracted—"made accommodations" with the enemy.

Mihailovich is dead and Yugoslavia nearly so. The upshot and ultimate fate of the only Balkan peoples to fight, deliberately and defiantly, on the side of the West was betrayal. (It should be added that the Greeks had been attacked the previous October by the Italians from Albania and that they gave a splendid account of themselves.) In the most calloused and cold-blooded deal in the history of the United States, Franklin D. Roosevelt and Winston Churchill at Teheran ceded to Stalin the right to impose a Communist dictatorship upon Serbia and Yugoslavia. This "Great Powers" deal stemmed back to January 1942, when the so-called "Curzon Line" was established, splitting Poland between the tender mercies of the German *Wehrmacht* and the political commissars of the Soviet Red Army. This powwow is too disgusting to recapitulate, although it must still haunt Mr. Churchill's waking hours, although not so vividly as the murder of Mihailovich.

Manchuria, Dairen and the Kurile islands were sold out later with Roosevelt at Yalta and Truman at Potsdam—although Chiang Kai-shek already had been lied to and betrayed at Cairo—and a reportedly repentant and now dead Roosevelt has since been represented by various and sundry Monday morning political quarterbacks as having been about to ask Stalin for an accounting of the shuffle.

But—*Yugoslavia*. The moral challenge of the Balkans would be as great as that of the Middle East were the Balkans not now a strictly military problem.

Yugoslavia is the major military problem. Here is what appears to be a considerable military force of some twenty-four divisions, largely supplied by the United States, under the leadership of Tito, who is popularly supposed to be in opposition to the Soviet. What appears to be twenty-four divisions allied with the West is mirage. American soldiers on the queasy Trieste front are perfectly aware of that. The Yugoslav Army is a mirage. War with Russia will split the army of south Slavs sixteen ways from breakfast, for the Serbs never will fight on the side of Tito. Nor will the Croats, without a decided advantage. Word from trusted Serbian agents— men trusted and true through the years of World War II—is that the Serb divisions of the current Yugoslav Army will take to the woods and mountains of Yugoslavia immediately upon the outbreak of war between Russia and the West, and wage guerrilla warfare in the tradition of the *Chetnici* and Mihailovich.

Civil war will result. Civil war in the Balkans is not pretty. It is difficult for Westerners to understand how deep hatred can go and how ruthless Balkan peoples can be. There are old scores to be settled, and settled they will be. The infamy of Croat treachery in World War II has not been forgotten. The Serbs are hard fighters, hard losers.

The infamy of the Western sellout of the Balkans is a trifle easier to take. Somehow, some way, the peasants of Serbia still believe in the ultimate integrity and honesty of the Western peoples. In this they are almost alone among the people of what, for military reasons, we call the Middle East. It is very difficult for this writer to understand—this bizarre loyalty to faraway peoples who were tried and found so dreadfully wanting when the blue chips were down. But it is easier to take. The Serbs are a rough and ready people who understand that Westerners, and Western Europeans, are soft and malleable—and they haven't had to fight lately, or if they had to, it was a pretty bad job.

Despite the so-called Iron Curtain, news seeps through to Yugoslavia. The underground is enormous and organized. Fighting men still need arms, but arms do dribble through. There is a hard core of resistance to Communism in Yugoslavia. Here are people inured by centuries of resistance to tyrants. Here are people steeped in a kind of fierce independence that has to be seen and experienced to be believed. One has to talk with them, individually, to know that the flame of revolt burns ever more brightly in Yugoslavia today.

As a war correspondent, I knew these people. I know them now. Barred from their country, with a price on my head, I nevertheless have talked to Serb agents and heard their stories. They are perfectly aware that war is coming and they welcome it. They welcome it as a surcease from bondage and terror, as millions of southern and central Europeans and Middle Easterners welcome it. War is no stranger. Our concern with the atomic bomb is a matter of puzzlement.

"What the hell?" they say. "You can die only once. What does it matter how?"

Once I remember driving back in a battered Buick from lower Dalmatia, across Hercegovina and Bosnia with the Croatian children on the roadside in the villages giving us the hated fascist salute. They had learned it from the Germans and the Croatian fascist *Ustashi* of the occupation troops. We came to the river, the Drina, and—as in the old song—we couldn't get across. The Serbs had blown the bridge to blazes. There was a primitive ferry, we were told, up the muddy, yellow, swollen river a piece.

We ground through the deep mud of Bosnia for perhaps four or five kilometers and I found the ferry crossing. It was one of those cable affairs and an ancient ferryboat and an ancient boatman who manipulated the oar to move the rickety boat in the flood tide of the Drina. Serbia lay on the farther bank. We had to wait for two gray German staff cars to cross first.

This was May 1941. Crossing, I talked to the old boatman. Things were rugged in Serbia, he told me. Villages bombed or burnt out. Churches destroyed. Women raped and children shot. The cattle were gone, driven off by the Germans, and the sheep. It was a blowy, dreary and utterly miserable kind of afternoon and the river was rough and muddy. I had left the old Buick to talk to the boatman and as we drew near the bank on the Serbian shore, Bob Macatee, the American First Secretary, called to me.

"Better get in!" he said. "Looks rough."

It did. The old ferryboat had nudged into the mud of the river bank. It looked knee-deep. It was thick, clayey mud.

"Drive 'er in, Bob!" I yelled to Macatee. I said goodby to the old boatman. We shook hands warmly. His gnarled palms were enormous.

"*Napret!*" he said. "*Forward!*"

Bob gave the Buick the gun and she slewed off the ferry and through the mud up the bank to the roadway. Bob was yelling for me to come on.

I took my time. I stepped off the clayey, slippery deck into the oozy, thick clay mud of Serbia. It felt good.

16

THERE IS SOMETHING OBSCENE in the deliberate falsification of any history, and the obscenity is trebled and felony compounded when great powers conspire to cloak their iniquities in the venal paper work of ghostly rewrite batteries. The entire history of the Middle East and the interlocking Balkans is stained with such perfidy, such faithlessness to fact. Where Hitler's wretched writing minions left off, Stalin's took over—with the aid, comfort and assistance of hosts of conscienceless or woolly-minded writers in the West.

The Balkans and the faraway lands of the Middle East are a dark and bloody ground and easy prey to the literary charlatans employed, or self-appointed, to mop up and gloss over the "mistakes" of the Great Powers which played fast and loose with the destinies of the Balkan and Middle Eastern peoples. And the game is still in progress.

The betrayal of Yugoslavia is the blackest chapter in the modern record of the United States State Department. Poland is a close parallel. Turkey, but for the grace of superb Turkish diplomacy and a tough-minded army, would have been sacrificed, too.

The mute, blind and stumbling aspirations of the Balkan and Middle Eastern peoples were stiff-armed, in the closing, critical years of World War II, with all the finesse and gentility of a Bronko Nagurski hitting right guard. Without the Poles, the Serbs of Yugoslavia, the Greeks and the Turks and the myriad handfuls of desperate guerrillas who rallied against tyranny in Southeastern Europe and the Middle East, the unholy Axis alliance might have prevailed. This is a very unpopular point of view, in Whitehall, Washington and Moscow, even today, but it is nonetheless accurate. In point of cold fact, there is a determined and concerted effort by the makers and wielders of Anglo-American and Soviet foreign policy to obfuscate the picture. It is appallingly reminiscent of the equally dark days of early 1939 when Republican Spain had fallen victim to Western apathy, lassitude and cowardice and delimited Communist objectives in Iberia and France.

In a word, the feathered obscenities of international falsehoods are coming home to roost in the Balkans and the contiguous Middle East. The battle-hardened Serbian leaders mistrust America only a little less than they despise perfidious British Balkan policy and only a trifle more than they hate Communist tyranny, in the sheep's raiment of Tito. Hungarian and Czech stooges are riding a Communist high horse of arrogance, but they and the Hungarian and Czech masses are perfectly aware that their present leaders will be unhorsed when it suits the Kremlin. The Bulgars, characteristically, hate and fear everybody, especially their immediate neighbors, the Serbs, the Greeks and the Turks. Utterly without shame or honor, Bulgaria's present-day governmental appointees would lay down their political portfolios for the assurance of an uninterrupted night's sleep.

Bulgaria's northern neighbor, Romania, is in her perennial prone position of a *nymph du pave,* a Latinized neo-Balkan whore who is desperately weary of the rough male kiss of Soviet Communism and wants *out!*—to found a new *mésalliance.*

Albania is of no political consequence and her technical control of the Strait of Otranto is *purely* technical. A pair of minesweepers and a really determined destroyer flotilla could neutralize Albania and the Albanians overnight. Albania's logical domination of the isle of Corfu is just as phony as her pretensions to the domination of Otranto. A determined Greek garrison can hold Corfu against the best Albania could muster.

Greece remains the one trustworthy Balkan ally of the West, and Greece, as sketched earlier, can become a defensive liability. Because of the strategic value of the Ionian Sea's approaches to Otranto and the Adriatic, Crete and the Sea of Candia, the Aegean and its islands and the approaches to the vital Dardanelles, Greece will be held, however, at almost all costs.

The Balkan peninsula is indispensable to any conqueror of the historic cradle of civilization in the eastern Mediterranean littoral. Yugoslavia's Vardar and Morava valleys upward from Salonika are traditional routes of conquest. And the Aegean, the Sea of Candia and the eastern Mediterranean opened outward to Soviet Schnorkel submarines would be suicidal to the U. S. Sixth Fleet and to the tankers, transports and supply ships to fuel and feed the enormous Western fighting forces which would be imperative in Middle Eastern war.

There is only one hitch, presently insuperable, and that is what this section of this work is all about. The enemy controls the Balkans, with the exception of Greece and European Turkey and, despite the genuine opposition of the bulk of these peoples to Soviet rule and exploitation there is no organized resistance. Resistance to tyranny is built on courage, cool-headed planning, audacity, hatred, and, sometimes, hope. And the irreducible minimum, arms.

There is no hope in the Balkans, outside of Serbia. Without this vital spark of hope there is no courage to implement the planning, and no boldness, and hatred withers of hunger and indecision and mistrust of faraway potential allies who talk endlessly and do little or nothing. The spark of resistance still glows in Serbia. It is nurtured and fanned by a history of centuries of bloody resistance to invaders, from the Middle East, Asia, Russia, Europe, everywhere.

Arms are lacking in Serbia for the genuine patriots. American allocations to Tito's Communist Yugoslavia have been enormous, however. The myth of "Titoism," like the myth of Mao Tse-tung's "agrarian reformists," has unlocked the floodgates of unwitting American arms and aid and propaganda to bolster a cruel and ruthless Communist dictator. The fictional obscenities fashioned upon the typewriters of Communist agents within and without the late and unlamented OWI and OSS persist in one form or another even today in the Western press and radio, and gullible or impressionable Senators and Congressmen and newspapermen visit Tito at Bled or Belgrade and come away with flattering pictures of this Balkan straw man. These posturings remind one of the obeisances of former U. S. Ambassador Joseph Davies before Stalin, or the fatuous relationship between G. Ward Price of the *London Daily Mail* and Adolf Hitler; between William Carney of *The New York Times* and Francisco Franco of Fascist Spain; or the pilgrimages of countless feckless Amer-

[151]

ican businessmen who were flattered by the receptions of Benito Mussolini.

The writings in the American press and leading American news and picture magazines of prominent trained seals, purporting to represent the true and unadulterated picture of Josip Broz, Tito of Communist Yugoslavia, further baffle and bewilder Serbian patriots. Their bewilderment is genuine. After all, Serb patriots were *there* when this Communist stooge was saddled upon their country by the Red Army. Most of them were *there* during the unrelenting war against the Axis forces of occupation. Nearly all of them have been *there* through the murderous regime of Tito. The outrageous fiction, parroted at an Overseas Press Club gathering, to the effect that Tito inspired and led the Serbian *coup d'état* of March 27, 1941, was dutifully reported and printed without comment in the American press.

On this occasion, *I* was *there*. Also on the scene in Belgrade was Arthur Bliss Lane, then U. S. Minister to Belgrade and later Ambassador to Poland during the notorious Anglo-American betrayal of the Polish State. It is a matter of record that Arthur Bliss Lane resigned, after more than thirty years in the U. S. foreign service, rather than rubber-stamp the Polish sellout, and wrote an eloquent book exposing the entire, shoddy deal. It is also a matter of record that this writer also tendered his resignation to *The New York Times* following the State Department-War Department-OWI-OSS betrayal of Mihailovich of Yugoslavia and that newspaper's editorial endorsement of Tito.

There is something most definitely obscene in the deliberate falsification of history. When the State Department of the United States and Soviet *agit-prop* conspire to falsify the history of the Yugoslav and Polish betrayals, and with the watered-down apologia of the British Prime Minister in the case of Yugoslavia, an observer hardly can foster blame upon the Balkan and Middle Eastern peoples for the fishy eye they turn upon the West.

The magnificent statesmanship and writings of Mr. Winston Spencer Churchill must be revered even today in the inner fastnesses of the woods and mountains of Yugoslavia. It was Mr. Churchill who uttered the memorable statement to the effect that the people of Yugoslavia had "found their soul" following the March 27 *coup d'état*. It was a ringing, orotund phrase, in keeping with Mr. Churchill's incomparable, dauntless marshalings of the English language in the darkest days of Hitler's triumphs on the Western front and over flaming London.

There was only one thing fundamentally wrong with Mr. Churchill's gratuitous tribute to Yugoslavia on March 28, 1941.

The Serbs of Yugoslavia had not found their soul. They had never lost it.

Nor have they.

It is well, in splicing the rhetoric of orators and writers, to piece it together for factual and historical continuity as well as admiration or criticism. Since this work deals specifically with the Middle East and the dangerous Balkans and the Asiatic and North African periphery, the following incident is highly pertinent, completely germane and absolutely verifiable by John Wallis of *Reuter's*, Dana Adams Schmidt, then *United Press* correspondent in Ankara and presently roving Middle East writer for the *New York Times;* Winston Burdett of *CBS* and Martin Agronsky, then *NBC* in Ankara and presently *ABC* from Washington. All of us were present at a press conference held by Sir Hughe Montgomery Knatchbull-Hugessen, the British Ambassador to Ankara (and the dupe of the notorious international spy, Cicero) during the critical war years of World War II. Also present was one of Britain's foremost diplomatic career men, Sir Geoffrey Harrington Thompson, then only "Tommy" and unknighted despite his superb work in wartime Spain, and later counselor at Baghdad, Ambassador in Bangkok and presently Ambassador at Santiago.

Again, it is a matter of record that the British Embassy and its Ambassador in Ankara, Turkey—one of the most crucial capitals in the world—were completely in the dark for twenty-four hours following Germany's assault upon Russia on June 22, 1941, as to whether Britain would commit herself to alliance with the Soviet Union. On the final record is the statement of Sir Hughe, via cable from London, in a direct quote from Mr. Churchill to the effect that Mr. Churchill, under the circumstances, "would shake hands with the devil himself."

Politics and war traditionally make weird bedfellows. Mr. Churchill and his son, Randolph, have been between the sheets of some extraordinary four-posters. Mr. David Low of New Zealand immortalized one of them with his incomparable pen. That was in the London *Observer* on June 23, 1941.

These political niceties and editorial marginalia cut very little ice, however, with the peoples of the Balkans and the Middle East. British arrogance and colonialism were not limited to India, Malaya, Ceylon and the Middle East in the dreadful years that the locusts of toplofty sahib mentality were devouring. Nor did the endless parade of American foreign-service incompetents rally any enthusiasm for Yankee influence out there. On the contrary. Our American envoys, for the most part, took the usual briefing from the local British wallah and turned up punctually for gin slings and a spot of bridge and confined their official activities to the greasing of commercial skids for the latest incoming freighters laden with American merchandise.

Until quite recently, and with extremely few exceptions, this situation prevailed throughout the Balkans and the Middle Eastern states. Arthur Bliss Lanes are very rare—and growing rarer. Either the American diplomats joined their British cousins in the petty palace intrigues, cocktail parties and soirees of the corrupt ruling classes—or they severely eschewed social contacts and lived in a social, diplomatic and political vacuum which also got them nowhere. Tough-minded consular officials who came out got the brush-off and took the hint, or they were transferred or given the slow-boat treatment home. Independent engineers, drillers, farm implement salesmen and aircraft representatives usually give American embassies as wide a berth as possible, even today.

Yet the largest inroads of power and influence and genuine friendship in the Balkans and the Middle East have been cut by these selfsame private citizens. "The Embassy Set" is a cussword in Middle East, as it used to be in most of the Balkans, a real epithet implying stuffed shirts, impossible, left-handed uxoriousness—or, more recently, and deadly seriously, the casual sleeping around characteristic of army posts, and downright homosexuality. This applies specifically at the moment to a segment of the American colony in Istanbul. Perversion of all fashions is commonplace in the Middle East, so generally accepted that the knowledge that it could have political leverage came as a bonanza to Communist operatives. The Turkish Sûreté, the secret police, ride herd on the "Bosporus Set" with unrelenting, contemptuous regularity. When the practices become too flagrant, the offender is notified that his or her visa is cancelled and the Communists look for a new operative.

These additional obscenities are an extra puzzlement to the hardy Balkan peoples. Mountain and woodland folk, they honestly do not understand the foibles of the people who frequent the fleshpots of Budapest, Bucharest, Belgrade, Istanbul and Athens. They *do* understand, however, the noisome political trade in women and men who are transshipped through the Iron Curtain, frequently with narcotics, aphrodisiacs and strange anaphrodisiacs, to Athens and Istanbul. The Hungarian trade in women via Athens is still flourishing. Bulgaria exports young men. Bulgarian women, as a rule, are singularly unattractive, barrel-shaped, big-footed and unwashed.

Hungary always has exported women. Opium is the lifeblood of drug addicts throughout the Levant, and the narcotics trade via Italy is a racket netting millions annually to Charles ("Lucky") Luciano and his combine. Athens streets swarm with teen-aged pimps eager to sell their teen-age sisters for a handful of drachmae. Istanbul licenses prostitutes and Beirut and Cairo have women who work both sides of the streets for anybody at reasonable prices.

What have they got to lose?

Roughly, nothing. If there is a conscience in the roiling Balkans, it lies deep in the heart of Serbia, far above the filth and the rottenness of the bazaars and market places. It aches in the minds of the teachers, lawyers, soldiers, priests, the progressive and professional men and women who have withdrawn from Belgrade and Skoplje and Cetinje, in Montenegro, and peered uncertainly toward the West for signs of assistance.

Russia has prepared its own brand of genocide for the Serbs, the only Balkan and Southeastern European peoples it cannot conquer. It is more subtle than the German burp-gun or gas chamber or the flaming churches and schoolhouses which consumed thousands of Serbs under the German occupation before the Communist Russian terror. Lidice, Czechoslovakia, is an interesting psychological phenomenon to the Serbs. Serbia had a score of Lidices, but badly publicized. The Serbs are extremely poor about advertising their dead. That is why the Russian brand of genocide has been so successful in Serbia. Serbs disappear, in dead of night, by ones and twos, never to be heard of again. Or rarely. They are an unimaginably tough people and sometimes they survive the northeast-bound cattle cars in subfreezing weather and beat their guards and escape. When they survive, they talk and talk well but sparsely. Mostly, now, they talk about a Serbia which they say will rise again. They have lost hope and faith in their king, Peter II of Yugoslavia, for they do not believe in a Yugoslavia and they do not believe any longer in the integrity of their king. Much of that faith was based in a kind of mysticism anyway. They could not understand the fact that young King Peter, a Karageorgevitch, could permit himself to be browbeaten into submission by a British policy and a British Prime Minister, Mr. Churchill, both of whom were intent upon sacrificing Serbia to a ravening Communist terrorism and dictatorship supplanting the cold-blooded murder and outright genocide of an Adolf Hitler. Not that they believe that was Mr. Churchill's intention, but as Serbs, they know history.

The history they know is unanswerable from the current international press box. Answerable, perhaps, in apologia and extenuating remarks, but as unanswerable to the embattled Serbs as the categorical imperative, the unconditional command of conscience.

The command of the political conscience is the most powerful force I have ever been privileged to witness. It must have existed in the Alamo with Crockett and Travis and Bowie and at Thermopylae and everywhere in the world since time began that men and women had to make up their minds whether to live in freedom, die, or wither in thralldom.

In the Balkans today lies one country, Serbia, devoted to liberty and unquestioning battle to achieve it. The Serbs are equaled only by the Turks beyond the Maritza river at the Bulgarian frontier in an unquenchable thirst for a freedom from the vicious menaces and the absurd promises which alternately have threatened and cozened the peoples of Southeastern Europe and the Middle East for centuries.

There is an old Czarist song we used to sing in the Balkans when our spirits were low, and mighty low they were in the drear days of 1941. The title was: "The Wind Is Blowing from This Side of the Carpathians and We and the Russians Are 200,000,000 Strong." It is probably one of the longest, and presently most meaningless, song titles in history, but the melody was good.

The Russians are vastly stronger today and the winds that blow from the Carpatho-Ukraine are spine-chilling to the hungry, encased peoples of the violent Balkans. There is no hope from the engulfing east and no faith there in the malingering west. In the Balkans there is one small, diminishing, guttering spark.

17

SEVENTEEN CENTURIES of war and invasion form the bloody backdrop for Balkan history since the Slavonic migrations which spelled the ultimate doom of the Byzantine rulers, and there is neither time nor reason here to indulge in the romantic traceries of races, religions and cultures which still influence the patterns of the current everyday lives of the oppressed Balkan peoples. Miss Rebecca West essayed this ambitious task in *Black Lamb and Grey Falcon* and these two large volumes are enthusiastically and almost unreservedly recommended by this writer to anybody sufficiently interested in Balkan folklore to plow through them. They are wonderfully rewarding reading.

The urgency of Balkan history at the intersections just beyond the turn of the twentieth century impel a stern and stubborn regard for traffic signals and the hazards of the road ahead. Balkan roadways, political or otherwise, are notoriously dangerous, ill-lighted and studded with pitfalls.

The guttering spark of Serbian intransigence is the only illumination in the blackness of what my longtime friend and colleague, Leigh White, accurately diagnosed in its tragic beginnings as *The Long Balkan Night*. White referred to the Axis invasion and occupation of the Balkan peninsula and the beginnings of Soviet hegemony as Anglo-American global strategy ignored this vital area and the inseparable Middle East. And Leigh White was right.

A genuine *shufti* (Arabic for "look-see") at this writing, however, necessitates a quick and hard-boiled look backward, at least through forty years.

Serbia inspired and led the first Balkan war against Turkey in 1912. Bulgaria, Greece and the Montenegrin kingdom completed the military alliance. Montenegrin irregulars actually started the shooting. Bulgaria reneged on divisional troop allotments and supplied only one division for the Macedonian campaign and the fighting on the Greco-Turkish frontier in Thrace, when six had been promised, but Turkey's twelve divisions ultimately were defeated. Bulgaria's troops in the eastern Thracian fighting were brilliantly successful, as well they might have been with their preponderant strength, but the Serbian armies triumphed in Macedonia and smashed ahead into Ottoman territory despite Bulgarian treachery. Greek troops outflanked the Turks on the Vardar and hurled them back into Salonika where they surrendered. Serbian forces, meantime, struck through Albania to the sea and destroyed the last Turkish strongholds at Janina and Scutari. Grecian forces were reorganized under Serbian command at Scutari and a final blow was set when Britain and France intervened. A new state, called Albania, was to be founded and Britain summoned the warring Balkan powers to London to rubber-stamp its birth certificate.

Turkey backed out of Europe, aside from terrain about Constantinople and Gallipoli. An uneasy peace prevailed. Tension mounted. Bulgaria struck, utterly without warning, against Serbia and Greece, and the Second Balkan War was on. Serbo-Greek forces sustained and repelled the Bulgarian surprise attacks and launched counterattacks via the historic Struma Valley as Serbian forces decimated the Bulgars in bloody fighting in southern Serbia. Opportunistic Romania had declared war and Romanians were advancing on Sofia. The Turks retook Adrianople. Bulgaria folded.

To capsulate the Balkan Wars in a few hundred words is obviously impossible and, just as obviously, will outrage the cruet-pepper-and-salt-and-sugar-bowl Colonel Blimps who, until recently, were still refighting the tablecloth campaigns of Khartoum and Mafeking. The point is, it roughs in the Balkan picture of late '13 to early '14 and prepares the canvas for the beginnings of World War I, another immediate Balkan work which began with Gavrilo Princip at Sarajevo in Bosnia.

The killing of Austria's Archduke Ferdinand was just as inevitable as the events which followed, including the unacceptable ultimatum to the Serbian kingdom, the Austrian attack, Czarist Russia's entrance into war, and the ultimatumbling of the Balkan states and the nations of the Middle East. If it had not been Princip's, another Balkan arm would have struck the blow for Balkan liberty.

The Salonika campaign and the fighting in the Middle East in World War I apparently are as obscure and abstruse to many Europeans and millions of Westerners as the vital campaigns of the Middle East and the neglected Balkan states during World War II which laid the groundwork and fortifications for the war to come.

The war to come. The acceptance of this idea is a horror to most Americans and nearly all Europeans and those Asiatics not yet engaged in actual combat. The fact that the political groundwork and military fortifications long since have been laid is presented by a United States Secretary of State as something shameful and unacceptable, as if these manifestations were astral and unrelated to earthly decisions. The indisputable fact that those earthly decisions ignored all, or very nearly all, of the *casus belli* of World War II and its continuing effects; that, on the contrary, peoples and principles consecutively were and are sacrificed by pretenders to world peace; that such heinous less-than-half measures still exist today: such facts are a challenge to all free men everywhere.

Particularly in the Balkans and the Middle East. War is a horror to people who have lived it much more than to persons who have only read about it, or young men who have been chunked, precipitately, into it for reasons quite beyond them, in war areas they never previously had heard of, and for which they are instructed and ordered to fight and die. And for which their instructors offer no logical or acceptable reason beyond their, the instructors', total inability to fabricate an explanation. And a man about to die wants to know *why?*

A maxim in writing and show business is to stick to the clothesline. The clothesline throughout *Blood, Oil and Sand,* in the intolerably hot and repelling areas of the Arabian peninsula, in Egypt, in Iran, in the craggy Taurus mountains or on the sprawling Anatolian plateau, or in the grim and deadly Balkans, or in the reaches of Pakistan and India, Libya, Tunisia and Morocco, is, in a sense, this selfsame *why?*

Seventeen centuries of violence and perfidy overlay the bloody Balkans. The peoples of the Middle East can trace the murder and rapine of their countries for centuries more. Corrupt governments and savage interlopers live still in these

[162]

areas, encouraged and abetted by Western interests which would sustain the indecision of the present for purely meretricious motives. But, more importantly, the ruthless imperialistic Soviets crouch on the frontiers of the Middle East and infiltrate their capitals as they already control the governments of the Balkans. Governments, so-called. Terror is the watchword and torture and murder are the truncheons of law enforcement and justice today in Yugoslavia, Albania, Hungary, Bulgaria and Romania.

Balkan justice always was swift and violent. This writer has seen it in action. Bulgarian terrorism was infamous before the Gestapo added its niceties and before the MVD moved in from Moscow with the refinements of all the terroristic secret police since the Cheka, through the unfortunate nights of Radek, the NKVD and Lavrentia Beria.

Stark terror stalks the Balkans and those areas of the Middle East where Communist operatives and Western cowardice and incompetence have combined to create a vacuum lacking human decency and honesty and, inevitably, have sucked in the rottenness and corruption of the sinkholes of Russia and the Levant. Not even the Turks have been proof against it, for one of the great problems of the Turkish Sûreté today is the unrelenting influx of Communist operatives.

The unfortunate thing about this is that almost nobody in competent office in the West has done anything about it. Nor can one convince Americans that the Balkans and the Middle East tonight live in the grip of such a terror and incompetency to act. The incompetency is ours, American, for the British have lived and dealt with Balkan and Middle Eastern terror and intrigue for years. The British are perfectly aware that, unarrested, Soviet aggression can and will take over the Middle East and the Balkans, but they are not quite sure that some

[163]

miracle cannot yet happen to stay the Soviet operatives. And mutual Anglo-American distrust has done nothing to solve this issue.

It is rather like a police reporter attempting to tell a shopgirl what human brains look like when somebody with a .45 has blown them all over the wall of an apartment; or an infantryman who finally tells his wife about the fundamental details of hand-to-hand combat, and turns her against him forever; or a Balkan or Middle Eastern writer who seeks to explain the Balkans and the Middle East to somebody who has never been there, or to somebody, the usual somebody, who has been to all the bazaars, mosques, cathedrals, cafés, theatres, restaurants, night clubs and hotels.

In the next chapters, this writer intends to cover the Balkan Entente and the earnest efforts of some genuine patriots and statesmen to establish a confederation of Balkan peoples and some nearby Danubian peoples who wanted real unity and trade pacts to make the whole works go.

There were earnest and well-meaning people between and before Coudenhove-Kalergi and Streit who dreamt about Balkan, Southeastern European and European unity. Ed Angly, a fellow-Texan, used to dream aloud about it in Paris in those days and nights of the so-called *Sitzkrieg* when we were waiting for the sure opening of the *Blitzkrieg*; and so did Webb Miller, a frustrated and highly successful correspondent, and Walter Duranty, who really loved the Russian people and hated the regime he had, perforce, become an apologist for; and Bill Bird of the *Sun* and Kim Philby of the *London Times*, and, in the Balkans, men such as Sam Brewer and Leigh White and Leland Stowe and even Cedric Salter of the *London Daily Mail*, then, who gave everybody the impression

[164]

of being a lounge lizard and a thoroughly calloused and cynical fellow, but wasn't, at all.

There were many others, some still living, and too many dead, but all thoughtful men of good will and all men who had become passionately concerned with the state of the world by living with it as only a working newspaperman can live with it. This needs explanation. No newspaperman, packing a Hermes or a Smith-Corona, can be calipered with a man packing a tommy gun or a hunk of explosive, for the man with the gun has but one objective and a limited life expectancy. A correspondent usually can pull out and usually does and, barring accidents, he usually lives longer and comes home to write or talk about it. And it is not true that the good ones get it first. Ernie Pyle, Eddie Neil in Spain, Jack Singer of INS, and Terence Atherton, who got it when he parachuted back into Yugoslavia, are men who proved the exception. Atherton, Neil, Singer (a youngster) and Pyle took all the calculated risks there were. Pyle and Atherton simply lived longer to enjoy them, if that is the word.

Because this is a work about the Middle East and the Balkans, it might be well to get back to the heart of the Balkans, Belgrade in Yugoslavia, and to Terry Atherton in 1941. This redheaded Irishman certainly was the ablest correspondent in the entire Balkans. The fact that he was a British intelligence operative only added to the inside information he had and to what often must have been the frustrating inability to use it. Atherton had a couple of White Russians, a brother and sister, working for him, and both of them shall be nameless. Atherton, at forty-four and vigorously intelligenced beyond his years, knew the fundamental rottenness of the government of Dragisha Cvetkovitch and Cincar-Markovich which sold out Yugoslavia to the Axis, but he could not say so publicly.

Barred from saying so, and pinned down as intelligence operative and newspaperman, Atherton managed to aid the Serbian revolt against the corrupt Cvetkovitch regime beyond all present publishable measure.

He died for it when he parachuted back into Yugoslavia a trifle more than a year later. Horribly. He was tortured with all the subtle refinements of the Pavelitch Croatian Ustashi gangsters, including the blowtorch. Eyewitness documents prove that Terry Atherton was still alive—a tough man—when his breastbone was torn from his body, after he had been revived from shock by ice water and injections of adrenalin. The Communist Croats wanted Atherton's information and directives, and wanted them bad. They did not get them.

It would seem to be a long way and centuries in time between the death in inquisition of a tight-lipped and tough British newspaperman and intelligence operative in World War II and the saga of Jovan Babunski. Jovan was a Serbian leader who killed his spate of Ottoman Turks and inspired the original verses of *Spremite, se Spremite, Chetnici,* one of the greater Serbian war songs, which are numberless. In the Balkans and the Middle East, however, centuries are telescoped in time and there are already songs and fables about Atherton, Marko (Tom Hudson, another Britisher who specialized in sabotage) and American airmen who parachuted into World War II Yugoslavia after Ploesti bombings to join the guerrillas in resistance to the Axis.

Seventeen complete centuries can intervene and yet there is the irreducible spark of resistance in Serbia. Where it came from and how it evolved and continued to live is a problem for the anthropologists. The vocal and documentary existence of Serbian resistance is as alive today as the last planeload of refugees at Idlewild or La Guardia or the ship in the North river. It is also morally inexpungable matter in the files of the Turkish intelligence service. The violent and bloody Balkans constitute an area inescapably linked to the vast, boiling Middle East and nobody knows this hard fact better than the Turks.

Largely because the Balkan areas are honeycombed today with "native" correspondents—that is, local correspondents who will file the official version of any interior happening to the UP, AP, INS and, occasionally, to the *New York Times*—a kind of paraphrase of news still reaches the West. It bears little resemblance to truth and is largely economic, because economic stories are easy to falsify for the general public and rock no political boats.

No writer can upset the Ministry of Propaganda with a story on some mythical new Five-Year Plan. Conformist correspondents are eagerly accepted, especially in Belgrade, where it has been demonstrated that Tito's Press and Propaganda Ministry will go to any length to keep the visiting firemen happy.

One cannot be subtle with a newspaper piece. Correspondents have tried it for years from areas under censorship, retroactive or direct. The newspaper reader either hasn't the time or doesn't give a damn for the shadings of opinion, either in syntax or punctuation. Brooks Atkinson of the *New York Times* also gave it a whirl from Moscow. Linton Wells essayed it, too, and Leigh White, Leland Stowe—and this correspondent, repeatedly. It would seem to be worth a try. It is not.

The hardest writing in the world cannot superimpose a slick and sleazy scrim upon the Balkan backdrop. The facts are now there, scuffed over but perfectly recognizable for all the world to see.

18

THE GALE OF THE WORLD, said Draja Mihailovich a short
few hours before his murder, had overswept him and
his work, and indeed it had, or was about to. There was nothing jocular about his statement, for such a man does not die
with a jocose remark on his lips. He looked back a long way.

The Balkan peninsula had been foredoomed to an additional
decade of bloodshed and tyranny under German jackboots
and Communist occupation from the time of the sellout of
Poland. Hungary and Romania had folded up, as early as the
turn of '41, under enormous economic, political and military
pressure from the Wilhelmstrasse and the Kremlin. Albania
had long been an Italian puppet and was now a tool of Axis
militarist explorations in Greece. The Russo-German nut-
cracker was exerting its squeeze upon Yugoslavia. Turkey
had been maneuvered into stubborn neutrality. The Middle
Eastern powers saw only the military might of Germany, the

[168]

obvious duplicity of the Soviets and the divided position of the unintelligenced West.

The Balkan peninsula today is in a similar position, with one major exception—Serbian Yugoslavia. In reverse. Bulgaria is Russian-occupied, controlled and operative as a Soviet Communist satellite. So is Romania. Hungary has an underground, but that underground is weak, unfed and uninspired. The Greeks are governmentally anti-Soviet, but the entire resources of the late ECA have been insufficient to persuade the Greek who has to go out and die for it that his current regime is worth the dying.

In a couple of paragraphs, the Balkans, a brief decade after, are as ripe for plucking as were the selfsame Balkans when very nearly prostrate or supplicating before Hitler. Excepting the Serbs of Yugoslavia. Resistance to Soviet tyranny is still there. What American policy and British financial, political and moral bankruptcy have accomplished in this vital area amounts, positively, to a cipher. There is no further valid excuse for bolstering a Communist dictator, Tito, for supporting a Communist regime which sustains the terrorist *camarilla* which, in turn, sustains Tito.

Yugoslavia encompasses some 96,000 square miles of ruggedly defensible terrain in strategic areas, and has about 16,-000,000 people. On the north, Yugoslavia is bounded by Austria, Hungary, Romania; on the south by Albania and Greece, with the long Adriatic on the west—and the narrow and explosive strip of Italian frontier. Yugoslavia's economy is at present agricultural, although her mineral deposits, including copper, are incalculable, and her forest preserves are enormous. Serbia's historical background is too well-known for recounting here. These fighting, dominant peoples of the Balkans are the only reliable Western allies.

[169]

Hungarian aspirations have been so battered by the Balkan gales that only a reasonably knowledgeable traveler in Southeastern Europe could know them, and still sympathize. Another Communist Balkan state in the logical grouping of Soviet satellites, Hungary is a perennial political whore. A producer of some of the most extraordinary writers and playwrights, second-rate premiers and first-rate restaurants and amiable women, Hungary once boasted political leaders. The religion is Roman Catholic to about 70 per cent. Public school education is allegedly compulsory and there are six (a seventh a-building) universities. Hungarian bauxite is good and plentiful and available to the highest bidder. The Hungarian economy still is hitched to agriculture and the great plains (or Alfold) area where sunlight and water abound. Budapest is a railhead and a major spy ring for the Soviets, as it was for the Nazis and, in World War I, for Germany.

Hungary is completely nationalized in the Soviet sense, as in the Hitlerian sense, and the country's agricultural production and industrial output are harnessed to the Soviet economic system. All farms are collectivized, insofar as possible, and Hungarian peasants who resisted the *kolkhozy* treatment were exported summarily.

Hungary's military strength is under five divisions at this writing, although the value of this supine Southeastern European state to the Russians in the realm of police work and communications is considerable. As under the minions of Himmler, and for precisely the same reasons, the MVD operatives of the Kremlin prefer Budapest to all Balkan capitals, and frequently move on to Beirut.

In other words, Hungary is a tool of the Soviet Union in all the worst senses of the word. Hungary's political aspirations have become so bastardized as to be unrecognizable.

The Vogeler case, which was materially defensible, and the case of the American fliers forced down in Hungary, which appears indefensible, only serve to bolster the case *against* the Hungarians at this time.

Cy Sulzberger of the *New York Times* thought the solution of Hungarian-Romanian hatred was a knife in the hand of every able-bodied Hungarian and Romanian. Cy's circa '41 solution was to build a wall around disputed Transylvania and let them go to it. This was sardonic humor, however unrealistic.

From the Middle East, Romania's political posture is so ridiculously and unhappily prone as to be dismissible. Like Hungary and Bulgaria, Romania tolerated corrupt rulers and feudal appointees to political office until the Communist intrusion was distantly acceptable. Romania's contiguity to the U.S.S.R. through Moldavia has been used by Romanians I have known for more than a decade as an explanation of political and military cowardice. Romanian politicos sought to explain the same cowardice in the days of Nazi aggression in Poland, and for the same reason.

One of the most potentially powerful states in Southeastern Europe, Romania is the weakest and sloppiest. Corrupt, obscene in the worst political and moral sense, Romania invited everything she got from her exiled monarch, Carol, his son Michael, Antonescu, and the rotters who intruded and supervened. Romania could have been one of the dominant powers of the Balkans with leadership. An area of 91,000 square miles, much of it arable; oil and waterways and virtual control of the Danube, the Carpathians and her strategic position, bordering Russia, Yugoslavia, Bulgaria and the Black Sea, could have made Romania one of the outspoken voices of the Balkans and the Middle East. No such voice even cleared its throat. Romania became a wartime and post-World War II prey to every form of vice and sordid commercialism, and the strumpet of Soviet commerce in the traffic of post-war Danubian deals in "hot" cargoes from the West.

Only Bulgaria tops Romania in genuine Communist filth of Balkan occupation. While Hungary is the major communications point for Communist operation, and Bucharest in Romania is the clearinghouse for the two-way traffic in westbound drugs and women and eastbound strategic materials for the Soviets, Sofia and Burgas are the real outlets for the slime and scum siphoned into neighboring Istanbul and, via the Black Sea, to Igneada and Midyea. Zonguldak also has its quota of whores, perverts and killers shipped to Turkey and the Middle East. Some of them slip off at Istanbul from the regular packet boats, but the traffic now is extensively screened by the Turkish police and few Soviet operatives get through.

Bulgaria could be one of the most dangerous areas in the world to the West. Because of Western failures in intelligence work and the astonishing disparity of viewpoints and liaison between the operatives dispatched, after careful training from Washington, many of these persons arrive badly briefed. What is worse, they get no briefing whatsoever from the Embassy.

Bulgaria goes on and so do its Communist operatives. Bulgaria is least dangerous where the Bulgars and Turks are concerned. The Turks have a special problem in dealing with ethnical Turks forcibly expelled from Bulgaria under the new Communist laws which order any Turk out of Bulgaria who cannot prove his right to Bulgarian citizenship. No Turk can do so. There were no passports centuries back when the Turks entered Bulgaria. The Turks screen ethnic Turks from Bulgaria carefully, but they cannot get all the operatives who slip through. Most of them they do, the important ones.

[172]

In condensing the Balkan phase of this work, the author can only plead indulgence on the part of the reader who checked in lately—historically, that is. The Balkans warrant much more coverage. For one reason or another, mostly classified, this is impossible.

The Balkan peoples are inextricably tied up geographically with the peoples of the Middle East and with Russia.

The Balkan peoples, aside from the Serbs of Yugoslavia, have been aligned against the West, and they will fight Westerners as bitterly as they have fought each other through the centuries. It is not at all a pretty picture, but then the Balkans is not, any more than the Middle East is.

Were Mihailovich alive today, he would not like what he might see in Bulgaria (where he served brilliantly as military attaché) or in Prague, and, certainly, not in his native Serbia. The Balkans is an unhappy place today, as is the bloody strife-torn Middle East.

It is born of casual indifference from the West, and may well die there, with us.

19

GREECE'S ANCIENT GLORIES cannot compensate the hard-boiled twentieth century for the Hellenes' current vassal statehood under American dollar diplomacy, nor excuse its latent Communism which could again overwhelm this strategic Balkan kingdom in any major Balkan and Middle Eastern blowup. Like a patient half-etherized on an operating table, Greece alternately has struggled for neo-independence, or relaxed and sucked in enormous quantities of anesthetizing economic aid which, in turn, continues to react as a kind of weird political catatonia upon the peoples and their quarreling, indecisive leaders.

Greece simply cannot make up its collective mind. And Greece's dreadful poverty is no spur to positive thinking and dynamic action. It can be argued most cogently that Anglo-American "imperialism" roughhoused the Greeks into their political strait jacket. It can also be reasonably debated that ravening, ruthless Communism and the unrelenting demands of sheer self-preservation forced armed British intervention and continued Western domination to repel Communism from engulfing this last strategic Balkan state.

Either argument, however, would beg the immutable question of Greece's genuine national aspirations. The first argument, of course, is Moscow's, and the second that of Whitehall and Washington. Both of them have reverberated endlessly via the world press and radio and in the U.N., and everywhere in Greece, where the peoples are undoubtedly the most talkative in the world. One can launch a violent political argument in Athens merely by remarking on the state of the weather.

Greece's political weather rarely has been more changeable than during the surcharged days and nights of '51 and early '52. Imitative of the French, and the Spanish in the frenzied days before the outbreak of the Spanish Civil War, the Greeks continue to divide and subdivide politically, making impossible any permanent national government and national unity.

Greece currently presents the West with its severest foreign economic aid problem and grave political and military conundrums at one of the toughest moments in modern history. In a relative nutshell: the small Greek nation fought gallantly and victoriously against the Italians in 1940 and collapsed under the might of Germany in 1941; and, bulwarked by comparatively large economic and military assistance, the semi-dictatorial government has aligned itself almost unreservedly with the United States in the great power struggle between Russia and the West in the Balkans and the Middle East. Greece's price for Western alliance, however, is a current cool $277,-000,000, which was slashed by Washington to $182,333,000 at the end of 1951. Greece's bargaining points comprise her theoretically strategic position and her small but able army and minuscule navy and air forces.

And her theoretically strong bargaining position as the last official major outpost against Communism in the Balkans. The stern fact that the outpost is hollow-shelled and is garrisoned largely by weak and dissident political leadership, sustained only by American aid and British threats and promises, is largely ignored by Washington. The Greeks, like the Iranians and the Egyptians and virtually all of the peoples of the reachable Balkans and the Middle East, desperately need genuine Point Four economic assistance, but assistance properly administered and supervised to avoid the sloth, indolence and indifference which have marked American assistance programs in nearly all of this area.

Neighboring Turkey remains a shining exception to the rule. It reflects the Turkish attitude that the Turks will fight anywhere, any time, aided or unaided, against outside aggression. This is not the attitude of Greek leaders who now maintain that Greece cannot defend herself unless the "disastrous cuts" in American aid are restored.

It is tragically true that military thinking has supplanted economic thinking in foreign aid from Washington, but it is also starkly true that this was the direct result of shoddy, incompetent administration from the top, in Washington and abroad, and that Greece is one of the prime examples.

Greece lies ruggedly and rockily upon the southern Balkan peninsula, about the size of Arizona, with a population of some 7,950,000 peoples, most of whom have a lean time of it even in the good years. Greece is bordered on the northwest by some of the most ferocious and unreliable peoples in the dark and bloody Balkans—the anarchic Albanians, the Macedonian irredenta of Yugoslavia (who maintain tribal relations, blood feuds and maraudings, political and otherwise, with Greek Macedonians and Macedonians in neighboring Bulgaria) and the treacherous Bulgars themselves, who are firmly in the Communist camp. Greece's eastern frontiers in Thrace are relatively safe with the friendly Turks, but Grecian Thrace would be a walkover for any determined northern invader. Greece's 8,800 miles of idyllic islands are a paradise for casual tourists and stonily unproductive for islanders and mainlanders, aside from the fishing. Less than one-fifth of the rocky Greek soil is arable. Olive and olive oil, dried figs, currants and raisins, cottonseed, sponges and lean-shanked cattle bolster the so-called peasant economy. Greece has no coal and her known iron, copper, lead, zinc and magnesium deposits are negligible. A trickle of ECA support, now coordinated under the Mutual Security Agency, has primed the pump for hydroelectric works along and around Greece's myriad lakes and rivers.

Stormy Albania towers craggily along Greece's northern frontier and is a periodic source of violence and political trouble. The tribal mountaineers of Albania cordially hate and fear all of their neighbors, including the Montenegrins of neighboring Yugoslavia and the Greeks and the Macedonians of both countries. With four seaports and two major airdromes, Albania theoretically dominates and controls the Strait of Otranto, but it is doubtful that the Communist Albanians could hold this inlet from the Ionian to the Adriatic against any determined assault. General Enver Hoxha is Albania's Communist-appointed dictator and recent reports indicate that the Russians have stepped up the building of new bases in the mountains. The Albanian population is estimated at about 1,800,000, scattered through the inaccessible mountains and down the cliffs to the narrow Adriatic and Ionian shores.

In a Baedeker Albania would deserve fuller treatment, if

only for the wild, combative history of its peoples and its forbidding terrain of black mountains, its blood feuds and ardent xenophobia. Albania remains merely a relative pinpoint, however, upon the periphery of the embroiling Middle East and the nearby, strategic Balkans, and served recently in world history only as a springboard for Mussolini's ill-advised plunge into Greece.

Strategically, Albania still threatens Greece as a Communist espionage center and a base of operations for the *banditti* who forage out of their mountain retreats to pillage in Yugoslavia and Greece.

The kingdom of Hellas cannot be dismissed so readily, nor has it been dismissed in growing Western defense plans for the Middle East, nor yet by the Russians apparently. But this writer has pointed out, in the study of contiguous areas such as Turkey and the islands dotting the Aegean approaches to the vital Dardanelles, that Greece has sometimes proved more a defensive liability than a genuinely strategic asset.

The very nature of the threatened conflict with Russia in the Middle East and the Balkans impels any conscientious observer to more than a cursory look at Greece's current assets and definite debits. Pentagon planners must map their potential defense, counteroffensives and over-all campaigns upon a very large number of assumptions. One such assumption, naturally, is a Balkan front against the Soviets, to prevent a forcing or aerial and naval blockade of the Dardanelles. This might entail a reopening of the famous Salonika front of World War I, hostilities in Thrace and, without doubt, extensive guerrilla action from both sides in the mountains and valleys, gulfs and bays and islands of Greece. Winston Churchill's memoirs, in his fifth volume, *Closing the Ring*, touch upon the enormous value which the British Admiralty and the British

Intelligence placed upon these areas, although they were never fully utilized by the eventual planners who committed the West to the prolonged and costly Italian campaign.

Europe *does* have a soft underbelly and a Russian-occupied Europe would be as vulnerable to Western attack from the Balkans and the vast Middle East as Nazi Germany might have been. One of the softer spots, properly probed and stabbed at the psychological moment, could be Salonika and the classical invasion route northward up the Vardar and Morava valleys of Yugoslavia. Control of most of Greece would be imperative to such operations. Contrariwise, Communist control of Greek strongholds in the mountains dominating the sea lanes to Salonika would be disastrous. And the reportedly massive Soviet undersea arm could wreak havoc upon Allied shipping in the island-dotted Ionian Sea, the Sea of Candia between Crete and the Greek mainland and the islands of the Dodecanese and the Aegean.

Athens' Piraeus harbor, controlled and adequately protected, could funnel enormous quantities of supplies to Allied troops engaged in Balkan fighting. Uncontrolled and unprotected, Piraeus harbor could be transformed into another inferno, as the *Luftwaffe* proved in the German campaign in Greece in May 1941.

None of these factors has been overlooked by the Greeks in their urgent demands for more and immediate assistance. Such necessities impelled even the laggard British Socialist Government and the malingering State Department to extend tardy recognition to the potential Greco-Turkish defensive bloc in the over-all planning of the North Atlantic Treaty Organization and the proposed Middle East Defense Command.

It is vastly past the hour in the Balkans and the Middle East today for hard bargaining by the West. Shrewd and honest administration of economic aid can perhaps stopper some of the gaping holes through which previous allocated funds have been drained away and siphoned off into ill-planned or downright crooked projects by inept or venal political appointees. Among Greece's nearly eight million peoples are many millions who earnestly desire aid to better themselves, not merely largesse or blackmail lest they go Communist.

Altogether too many Western envoys, diplomatic and commercial, have exposed themselves, however, as notoriously incompetent in their delicate dealings with the Balkan and Middle Eastern peoples. This has been particularly true in Greece in a period which has been shown to have been perilously short.

The military exigencies are another matter, although directly related insofar as Congressional appropriations are concerned, and inescapably involved in the melancholy state of Anglo-American planning and operational liaison throughout this gigantic area. Sudden war with the Soviet would scrub most of the current differences over responsibilities, commands, and petty matters of protocol which still engage an altogether disproportionate amount of time and attention between British and American Army and Naval personnel in many Middle Eastern posts. Sudden war, however, would also find a chaotic state of unpreparedness and disunity and, in many cases, a fatal lack in standardization of arms and even intelligence directives.

Such failures are highly unlikely among the thoroughly standardized potential enemy.

It is all very well for Administration leaders to sound off in grandiloquent speeches which purport really to examine the emergencies which compel economic and military aid to European, Middle Eastern and Asiatic peoples. And the prepared addresses of numberless beribboned and polished Army officers, and their civilian opposite numbers in the Defense Department, may sound well to most Americans.

Such talk has a hollow sound in the Balkans and the Middle East today and, from what this writer has gathered from competent correspondents in other theatres, in much of Western Europe and nearly all of Asia. While visiting Congressmen and Senators may *tsktsk* the foreign governmental corruption which is alleged to be almost entirely responsible for the essential breakdown in the American economic aid program, and grave hitches in the military preparedness of potential allies, the cold, unpalatable truth lies somewhere in between.

In rounding off the Balkan periphery coverage of this work, this writer takes the option of citing a Serbian patriot recently quoted by Arthur Bliss Lane, former United States Minister to Yugoslavia and Ambassador to Poland, who returned to Yugoslavia to see if the situation there was as dreadful as reported by the underground.

It was. Mr. Bliss Lane, a tough-minded U. S. career diplomat who indignantly resigned from the State Department after more than thirty years of service, found American policy in Yugoslavia supporting still another dictator in the enslavement of a people. Inasmuch as he had been in Yugoslavia at the outset of the gallant Serbian revolt against a corrupt and venal government, and through the beginnings of the Yugoslav resistance to Nazi terror and tyranny, Mr. Bliss Lane could assay and bitterly appreciate what "Titoism," so-called, is doing to Yugoslavia. Even more bitterly, he could recall that it was American policy which abandoned and betrayed the Serbian martyr, Mihailovich, and saddled Serbia and Yugoslavia with a Communist dictator. Mr. Bliss Lane now was seeking to dissuade a Serbian patriot from his expressed and blazing desire to come to America to tell Americans of Yugoslav descent, in the Serbo-Croat language, about the dangers of Communism and the terroristic dictatorship of Tito. Mr. Bliss Lane warned the Serb that the Serb's wife and children would be endangered as virtual hostages in Yugoslavia by any such undertaking.

The Serb replied: "You Americans, who have not lost your freedom, do not understand what freedom is. Only people who have lost their freedom can appreciate its value. We Yugoslavs, who have lost our freedom many times, know what freedom is and we know that, not even excepting one's own family, there is nothing more precious in the world than freedom."

Many of the legislators in the West and many of the world's speechmakers might give that quote a second reading.

They could even paste it in their hats.

20

FROM THE SULLEN, TRUCULENT BALKANS to the blazing Gulf of Aden and northward through the sheikhdoms of the Persian Gulf, bearing northeastward via Pakistan, Afghanistan's Hindu Kush, contested Kashmir and tiny Nepal in the Himalayas is a journey to a different world, and almost to the roof of it. It is a world of violence without end, of murder and intrigue and tremendous history in the making, and its myriad peoples around the Middle Eastern periphery can no more escape involvement in the exploding crises over more than 2,000,000 square miles than can the venturesome but fumbling West.

This is a nagging, nauseous thought to many a queasy Westerner. Old Middle Eastern hands have lived with this dread knowledge, however, for the building years of this unrelenting tension, and the tougher men have survived. No such survey and report as this one can ignore even the small but strategic Imamate (theocratic) ancient kingdom of Yemen, which lies in a triangular wedge at the faraway corner of the southern Red Sea and the Gulf of Aden. The Yemen's over-all terrain is vague, for its northern and northeastern frontiers fade, mirage-like, into the trackless and sandy, rocky uplands of Saudi Arabia and the Great Sandy Desert. Yemen is estimated at roughly 80,000 square miles of hot uplands and mountainous country and harbors about 3,500,000 devout Moslem peoples who grow coffee and grain, tan hides and dig in the rocky soil for precious stones. The capital is Sana, a walled city with eight gates, and the capital city and many oases were ravaged late in the summer of 1951 by cholera, which is an omnipresent threat in this isolated area.

Aden itself and the Aden Protectorate constitute a British Crown Colony exporting cigarettes and salt via Aden's fine harbor. The Colony proper, Aden, numbers some 96,000 residents, while the Protectorate includes another 815,000 seminomadic Arabic traders, peasants and saltmakers. The highly brackish sea waters are flumed into shallow seaside troughs where the baking sun evaporates the water and leaves the salt deposits.

The best and fastest and sturdiest racing and working camels in the world are bred just northeast of the Aden Protectorate in the desert Sultanate of Muscat and Oman which sprawls for more than a thousand miles along the lower edge of the Arabian peninsula from Ras Sajir on the Arabian Sea to Qatar on the Persian Gulf. Dried fish, limes, dates and pomegranates, with Arab bread, goat cheese and lamb are standard fare. The seaport of Muscat is the only major waterway outlet and most trade is with India, in fabrics and foodstuffs and the exchange, as in the Yemen, is in Maria Theresa dollars and Indian rupees. Inland, the intransigent Arabs fought for more than seven years and ultimately beat down the tax-collecting representatives of Saiyid Said bin-Taimur, who rules the coastal plains area from Muscat.

The sheikhdoms of Qatar, a fat finger jutting into the Persian Gulf, the Bahrein Islands and the realm of Sheikh Abdullah as Salim-as-Sabah, extend up the Persian Gulf to the muddy, crocodile-infested headwaters of the Shatt-al-Arab river, southward of the confluence of the ancient Tigris and Euphrates, and the Iranian oil crisis has focused white-hot attention upon this already sweltering area of the world. While Bahrein wells have been steady producers for years under Anglo-American supervision and protection, and the island's sheikhdom itself is "independent" under official British protection, it is the stepped-up production of the new oil strikes on Qatar which have led oil-hungry engineers southward for further drillings in these desolate sandy wastes.

Kuweit is a tiny sultanate covering less than 2,000 square miles, but this little wedge of hot, sandy desert with American and British engineers and Western production methods is producing nearly 32,000,000 barrels of high-grade crude oil per month. Known reserves in the Kuweit fields—and the new Magwa field—top 15 billion barrels. Sheikh Abdullah as Salim-as-Sabah is a generous monarch, and he can well afford to be. He receives his country's entire oil royalties before taxes and before shipment from the Kuweit jetties (which are able to load ten tankers at once), and his estimated income during 1952 will be more than 140 billion dollars. Small wonder, then, that forcibly enlightened British and American governmental and company operatives in Kuweit have joined with the Sheikh in a vast program of free hospitals, free schools, sanitation works and Western-made products which already have transformed life in this otherwise arid and miserable Persian Gulf kingdom into something like a paradise for its more than 132,000 peoples. Kuwait's trade prior to the new oil bonanza was largely with neighboring Iraq, Iran and the southerly Arab coast, in dried fruits and hides, and in pearls with India. Oil today supersedes everything in the lives of the dazzled local peoples, the foreign residents in the trade and the immigrant Arabs who are flowing into rich little Kuwait by every arriving *dhow* and from the still barren desert lands of the south. Trained Iranian operatives are seeking permission to emigrate from their once happy sinecures with the shutdown Abadan refinery and the oil fields, but official Iranian decrees have forbidden them. As usually happens in the Middle East, the official ukase is blinked at and only the shortage of tankers and docking facilities prevents the Kuwait field and the giant major producer—Burgan's installations— from topping more than a million barrels per day alone.

Little Yemen joined her giant and dominant neighbor, Saudi Arabia, and Egypt, Iraq, Syria and the Lebanon in the formation of the Arab League in 1945. The smaller sheikhs and sultans of lower Arabia and the Persian Gulf area had demonstrated no desire for mutual solidarity agreements or defense pacts, Arabic or otherwise, until recently. The Iranian crises and the Anglo-Egyptian clash had their repercussions throughout Araby and echoed eastward as well as west, however, and the ferment of Arab nationalism inflames even such distant and isolated peoples as these nomadic peoples scattered along the Gulf of Aden, the Arabian Sea and the Gulf of Oman. Sheikh Abdullah of Kuwait and his peoples could hardly escape some of the blast from the Iranian oil-and-nationalism explosion almost on Kuwait's doorstep, but the sheikh is temporarily content with his fabulous royalties which continue to mount with every passing day. The longer Iranian oil fields are shut down and the refinery idle, the longer will tiny

[186]

Kuweit continue to fatten financially and emerge ultimately as a political power to be reckoned with.

Eastward across the troubled stretches of southern Iran lies Pakistan, or its better half comprising the Punjab, the Northwest Frontier Province, Baluchistan and the Sind. By no stretch of geographical relationship, by no direct economic or political interests, nor by any febrile stretch of even Russian imagination, could Bengal, Assam and the smaller, former princely Indian states which make up the Eastern Dominion of Pakistan be considered a part of the Asiatic periphery of the great Middle East. The western and greater half of the Dominion of Pakistan is as concerned with the greater Middle East as is Afghanistan and even Nepal along the Tibetan border.

Following the partition of the Indian subcontinent in mid-August 1947, Pakistan retained Dominion status in the British Commonwealth. India proclaimed itself a republic. The partition had been seized upon, of course, as the only readily workable solution to the otherwise insoluble problem of Pakistan's predominantly Moslem population and the Hindu majority in India. When Pakistan moved to annex Kashmir, which is 77 per cent Moslem, Kashmir's Hindu Maharajah protested and got aid from India and among Hindu followers within the country. Civil war followed. U.N. intervention secured a cease-fire, but the issue still hung in doubt in early 1952.

Should the status of Pakistan and her quarrel with India seem remote from the emergencies affecting the Middle East, it is handy to remember that Pakistan is a huge country of some 360,000 miles with an aggressive, Moslem population of an estimated 77 millions and some of the best fighting men who ever enabled the British to dominate India. Pakistan's political outlook is alert and independent and her voting record in the U.N., since her admission to membership in September 1947 has reflected a surprisingly strong grasp of *Weltpolitik*.

Karachi is Pakistan's capital, a large seaport and the largest airport in all Asia. Western capital and influence have made great and increasingly beneficent inroads and almost every incoming plane among the fifteen international air lines which serve Karachi carries surveyors, engineers and contractors armed with ideas or blueprints for further extension of Pakistan's already extensive communications system of roads and railways, and improvements of her vast irrigation system which is the oldest and second largest in the world.

More than 80 per cent of Pakistan's population is agricultural and for the most part successfully so. Rice and wheat cover some 36,000,000 acres and the jute production is the world's largest. Engineers are probing geological surveys which have revealed large and rich veins of coal, sulphur, chromite and oil.

The educational system is extensive and growing, and Pakistan is proud of Punjab University in Lahore and Sind University in Karachi, where an impressive number of young men are cramming courses designed to fit them for diplomatic careers in the service of their government.

Almost, but not quite, Pakistan joins frontiers with the Soviet Union, near the towering juncture of the mighty Hindu Kush and the Himalayas. A narrow strip of neighboring Afghanistan and Kashmir itself intervene. At no point does Pakistan rub elbows with Communism. Communism has made definite progress among Hindu youth in India, and the movement was enormously encouraged during the peculiar political roundabouts of India's Premier Jawaharlal Nehru and his U.N. ambassador, Dr. Benegal Rau, during the midway period

[188]

of the Korean struggle. Communism had made few strides in Pakistan before the Indo-Pakistan partition and, after the severance, the Pakistanis cleaned house in earnest.

The assassination on October 16, 1951 in Rawalpindi of Pakistan's Premier Liaquat Ali Khan was blamed by Pakistan Leftists, Indian leaders and Communist spokesmen everywhere upon alleged Afghanistan terrorists. The killer himself was an Afghan, Said Akbar, but extensive investigation established the fact that he had been paid and armed by terrorists who only a few weeks before the slaying had been in conference with the Haj Amin el Husseini, the former Grand Mufti of Jerusalem, and Akbar's associates had been identified as Communist agents. To this writer's certain knowledge Liaquat Ali Khan vigorously opposed the rising Moslem fanaticism and terrorism in Islamic countries and was seeking a moderate solution through every means at his disposal to aid in the settlement of the thorny Iranian and Egyptian problems. Like the Turks, the Pakistanis are great warriors, but like the Turks they have learned some lessons from their endless history.

Al Haj Kahwaja Nazimuddin, successor to the murdered Premier, brought with him a reputation of temperance—nonalcoholic, in the true Moslem tradition—and in political affairs as well. He is an enormous man of considerable wit and excellent diplomatic and political training. A lawyer by profession, he entered politics at twenty-two and rose through the old East Bengal government to the portfolio of Premier. The new Prime Minister is reputedly a man of large private wealth and, despite his bulk, an ardent hunter.

Above all, he is known among his fellow cabinet ministers and to the king as a firm anti-Communist who is abundantly aware of Russian designs upon vulnerable areas along the uncomfortably nearby Afghanistan border points. Afghan warriors since 1947 have been agitating along the Pakistan border for creation of a separate tribal kingdom comprising followers of a movement for a free and independent Pushtunian realm. The Pushtus or Pathans are the fiercest of the Moslem fighting men in the craggy and historic border country between Afghanistan and what used to be British India. Pushtu tribesmen, and others, are reputed to receive in the neighborhood of nearly $10,000,000 a year to dissuade them from banditry. This figure is understood to be a trifle exaggerated.

Pakistan's king, Mohammed Zahir Shah, is not an immensely popular favorite, but governmental figures believe that his precipitate removal might be an invitation to the nearby Russians to undertake an adventure via Afghanistan, with the aid of the Pushtus.

Pakistan has been handed the ancient British mace as guardian of the historic Khyber Pass. Whether the intruder be Afghan or Russian, the Pakistanis are ordered to shoot to kill, and go on killing. Reputed the sharpest riflemen and the craftiest mountain fighters in the world, with the possible exception of the recently untried Swiss, the Pakistanis and their 40,000 troopers and irregulars should be able to arrest anything but a major invasion by Communist forces. Having marched in wartime with Pathan regulars of the British Army, this writer would compare them most favorably with the fierce little Gurkhas of neighboring Nepal, the Serbs and the Turks as among the most formidable combat troops anywhere.

The remote and mountainous pancake-shaped kingdom of Nepal actually is larger than it looks from below its Himalayan heights—some 50,000 largely uncharted square miles—and supports a population, also largely uncharted, of some 7,000,-000 peoples, mostly Hindustani. Nepal is bordered on the

[190]

north by Communist-dominated Tibet and on the west by Pakistan. Nepal now boasts airdromes, electric lights, buses, a movie theatre and, of course, that perennial challenger to all world mountaineers, Mount Everest, which towers over the capital of Khatmandu from fifty miles away.

Gurkha troopers form the bulk of the Nepalese army of 20,000 men, but Nepalese spokesmen assert that an irregular force of thrice that number could be mustered overnight. The Gurkhas are nearly all under five feet high, a blood mixture of Mongol-Hindu parentage. They are bland, almost totally expressionless, and in the British tropical uniforms they wore through the Middle Eastern campaigns of World War II, complete with Aussie-styled campaign hats strapped up on the side, they looked like nothing so much in the world as troops of Boy Scouts. The comparison ends there. One could as well compare the deadly, tiny, beautiful banded *krait* of Burma to the common garter snake. The Gurkha's pride and joy is his *kukri*, a razor-sharp curved knife which is worn on the belt in the precise center of the trooper's back. It was with the greatest difficulty that British officers used to be able to restrain Gurkha troops from abandoning their rifles and automatic weapons in order to close with the enemy using only the *kukri*. At trench warfare, infighting and patrol work, the Gurkha can be compared only with the American Indian for stealth, savagery and a miraculous ability to get back to base. It is the solemn tradition of the devoutly religious Gurkhas, and their fighting codes are bound up with their Buddhist beliefs, that the *kukri* never can be drawn without shedding blood.

There was an incident at Karachi which illustrates the point. A visiting general of top prominence had been flown in from an Asiatic base on an inspection tour of American installations. Fascinated by the snap and precision of the Gurkha security guard, the general circled the squad on the runway near our plane and espied the ramiform *kukris* glittering from the belt on the back of every pint-sized trooper. The general halted before the squad leader and spoke to him, in English, of course. The Gurkha, knowing only Hindustani, was impassive. He simply braced more stiffly. The general put one arm out and, leaning over, tapped the haft of the *kukri* in the belt on the trooper's back. Standing some fifty feet away, I had only half-witnessed the byplay.

"*No*—General!" I hollered. "Sir!——" It was too late. The little Gurkha trooper smacked his Lee-Enfield into his left palm and in one lightning movement came up with his *kukri,* which he presented in a perfect salute abaft his nose.

The general had wheeled on me between choler and bewilderment.

"What the *hell*—" began the general. I gestured mutely. The general turned. Our Gurkha trooper had lifted his left thumb from his butted rifle, sliced it neatly open with his *kukri,* and, with one continuing motion, returned the gleaming knife to its assigned place on the rear of his belt.

The general turned away and motioned his staff to enter our plane. He was mopping his brow and not, I thought, entirely from the sticky Karachi heat. From the window of the C-54, I could see the little Gurkha security trooper still stiffly at attention, a spreading pool of blood in the hot sand beside his boot.

Until about a century ago, according to understandably cloudy Nepalese history, Gurkha hill clans had ruled most of Nepal. With the alliance of tribal chieftains, Hindu Rajputs came in. There is a ten-member cabinet in Nepal today and

[192]

King Tribhubana Bir Bikram who came out of exile in 1951 to re-establish himself upon the gaudy Nepalese throne.

Nepal is seeking more Point Four assistance from the United States. One $50,000 allotment has been received in Khatmandu and an American agricultural worker, accompanied by a health expert, are reported in the interior during 1952. Matrika Prasad Koirala, Nepal's Prime Minister, expressed himself as enthusiastic about American economic aid, but also urged the United States to send in modern weapons for use against potential aggression from Russia.

Great little country.

21

Towering massively skyward at the northeasternmost fringe of the Asiatic Middle Eastern periphery, Afghanistan's mighty Hindu Kush glowers downward upon Red China, disputed Kashmir and Pakistan, southern Russia and strife-torn Iran, and mistily obscures some of the blood-thirstiest and most warring history of 2,000 years at a traditional, forbidding mountain crossroads. *Jahansuz*—"the World-Burner"—is the Afghan cognomen bestowed upon one of this fierce country's mightiest hero-villains, Alauddin Husain, who avenged his brother's death in 1153 by putting the torch to the mighty city-state of Ghazni and slaughtering every inhabitant who failed to flee into the Punjab.

A mere eight centuries later, as the Islamic clock turns, Afghanistan and its twelve million fierce peoples stand embattled at almost the selfsame crossroads dominating some 250,000 square miles of some of the ruggedest rocky soil on earth. Squarely athwart Russia's most direct route to Pakistan and the Khyber Pass to India, the indomitable and belligerent Afghans hate and fear the Communist U.S.S.R. as they hated the British Empire, and they fear and mistrust the Pakistan Dominion, despise the indecisive Kashmiri, and look with jaundiced eye upon Soviet and Anglo-American adventures in Iran upon Afghanistan's wild western frontiers. And well they might, for the written and legendary history of the Afghan peoples is one continuous tale of treachery, perfidy and foul play, sedition, murder, invasion and pillage—a trail of broken pledges, forgotten promises, torn-up treaties, and a succession of rulers who subjected their predecessors to every refinement of extinction from blinding, maiming, stabbing, poisoning and burning to the swifter, modern means of fire-arms.

Why any emboldened conqueror would desire Afghanistan is, outwardly, a real conundrum. The hard fact that recorded history shows more than 2,000 years of invasion and almost unremitting internecine struggle compels a closer look at what has been until recently a very foggy, mysterious and highly romanticized picture. British military history is studded with the names of colonial campaigners and the brilliant ribbons and medals awarded to British fighting men who fought, and died in legions, in an effort to perpetuate the legend that the sun never sets on the Empire. In the Hindu Kush, the sun rises late, burns fiercely and sets early. While most of Afghanistan lies above 4,000 feet, the Hindu Kush mountains dominate the capital, Kabul, from 14,000 to 15,000 feet and zoom upward to the north and northeast, within a couple of hundred miles, to more than 25,000 feet. It is a wild and unregenerate country of man-killing heat, mountain cold, limitless uplands and desert wastes, with no railroads and only rugged roads and ruggeder pathways through the windswept mountain passes. Afghanistan's three rivers, the Oxus and the Kabul in the northeast and the Halmand in the southwestern basin which opens outward through the center of the lower country, provide irrigation enough only to keep the most determined nomadic herdsmen and peasants on the roughest of fare. Banditry is still common, chiefly for wool and skins and cattle, and punishment is traditionally the same as in most remote areas of the Islam world. A minor thief merely has his hand chopped off, the right one. A major thief who steals a horse, gold or a really valuable female is put to death.

What, then, has inspired outsiders to risk their captains and legions in this cruel, forbidding land at what used to be considered one of the ends of the earth? Sheer curiosity, perhaps, at first, although Afghanistan's strategic mountain passes led invaders from the east, the Mongols and the Seljuk Turks notably, as surely as magnets. The predatory Afghans themselves naturally invited reprisals by their periodic pillaging expeditions into neighboring territories. As early as 200 B.C. Greeks and Islamic invaders struck inward from the west, and the rocky, sandy soil of the Afghans was drenched with the blood of the invaders and the defenders for centuries to come. Genghis Khan led his Mongol hordes down from the northeast and was ultimately expelled only by Tamerlane who established his headquarters in northern Afghanistan in the early part of the fourteenth century. India's Mogul Empire overwhelmed Kabul and the neighboring provinces and the conquering Persians moved in from the west. The Afghan Durrani and Ghilzai tribesmen rose in revolt against both invaders around 1737 and, for the first time, Afghanistan began to assume a kind of wary, treacherous unity.

Alarmed by the intrigues of Napoleon in Persia in 1809, the British East India Company dispatched one of its operatives into the wilds of Afghanistan to buy or barter for British security against the operations of the European adventurer.

A scant quarter century later Czarist Russia was menacing the Middle Eastern perimeter, and the British East India Company rushed another agent to Kabul in an effort to checkmate the Russians, who had already installed a mission in the Afghan capital. If this pattern begins to sound familiar to many Westerners, it is only the beginning of the whole warp and woof of ensuing history to the present. The first famous "Army of the Indus" was ordered into Afghanistan. That was in 1838. Numbering some 20,000 men, it swept triumphantly through the mountain passes, slaughtering unorganized Afghan rebels as they rose from their rocky heights to oppose the invasion. The British took Kandahar, stormed Ghazni and occupied Kabul where they established a "friendly" government. Capsulating events familiar to students of mid-Asian history, this account has time and space only to report that the Afghans rebelled, slew Sir William Macnaghten, the British special military envoy, and then violated a truce to wipe out to the next to last man some 700 British officers and soldiers, nearly 4,000 Indian troops and between 5,000 and 7,000 native conscripts who were put to the sword or joined the rebels. This massacre opened the bloody campaigns of the British and the Russians in Afghanistan, and for awhile Czarist Russia and the hard-pressed British found themselves allied in suppressing the redoubtable hillsmen.

Afghanistan's perilous position throughout most of World War I resulted from the alliance of Turkey, the Islamic spiritual leader, with the Central Powers and the increasingly anomalous positions of Britain and wavering Russia. It was at about this time that the Afghan ability to maneuver politically and diplomatically upon an international scale first was recognized in the West and in Russia. Afghanistan successfully surmounted, behind a formidable force of her irregular but highly effective mountain warriors, three successive "incidents" with the Russians, Italy and the troublesome British.

Briefly: Russia demanded consular rights at Ghazni and Kandahar and the Afghans refused, with the reasonable argument that such Russian outposts obviously were intended as centers of intrigue, espionage and sabotage for operations in India. Russia made warlike noises, but the Afghans stood firm and the Russians yielded. An Italian subject named Piparno was arrested in 1924 on charges of murdering an Afghan frontier policeman. Tried and sentenced to death, the Italian's cause aroused an outcry in Rome and the Italian Government sent notes bordering upon ultimatum. The Italian was summarily executed.

The murder of two British officers followed by the slaying of an Englishwoman and the kidnaping of her companion, allegedly by Afghan subjects, provoked renewed trouble with the British. The Afghan government rounded up the suspects, refused British demands for their extradition, and ultimately executed them. That was that.

Kiplingesque disregard for Middle Eastern and Asiatic peoples already was doomed, had British colonial policy not been too blind and too supercilious to recognize it. India continued to knuckle under for almost a quarter century more, but the stiff-necked and remote Afghans had set a pattern for their combative neighbors in present-day Pakistan, and the pattern was observed and followed. Afghan legations in London, Moscow, Berlin, Paris, Rome, Teheran and Ankara were staffed with tough-minded missions which were light on politesse but extremely quick in their ability to recognize right from wrong, and who unfailingly to this day emulate their warlike ancestors when they are subjected to indignities, political or personal.

An illustrative anecdote concerns a former United States Ambassador to a certain Middle Eastern country who, grudgingly, had been forced by the demands of diplomatic protocol to invite the Afghan Minister to the Embassy residence for a large, official dinner. The Afghan Minister was a genuine rough diamond, a real favorite with those of us among the correspondents' corps who knew him well. True, his French was atrocious (he spoke no English), and he was a two-fisted drinker, a prodigious eater (with both hands), and he sometimes shocked the ladies of the diplomatic corps by openly admiring what they displayed so freely in their *décolletage*.

On this memorable evening, and the following day, the American Ambassador followed what had become standard operational procedure under the iron whim of his wife, a wealthy but highly frugal woman who must have (had she known it) retarded the American envoy's career by a score of years or more. This good lady instructed her staff to pour cheap, new wine out of old bottles and domestic brandy out of Armagnac bottles, but only for certain guests seated at lower positions about the dinner table. This had been the lady's practice in previous posts, some of them in capitals where vintage wines and fine cognac were considered prohibitively expensive. Invariably, the suffering diplomats far down the protocol list had grinned and borne it. The Ambassador, himself a wealthy man, had protested this practice to no avail.

On the evening of the dinner, this writer, arriving early to check a late-breaking foreign-office development with the American envoy, overheard the end of an argument between the Ambassador and his wife. The Ambassador was just losing. The phony wine was being decanted.

"That Afghan *beast!*" hissed the lady. "He'll never know the difference!"

It was with special interest that I watched the Afghan Minister at dinner that evening. He wolfed the soup course with relish, meanwhile finishing the double scotch he had brought to the long table. His portion of the soufflé disappeared in a twinkling. The entree was prime ribs of beef and the lusty Afghan had tucked away two giant portions before his wine was poured. The swarthy mid-Asian diplomat then lifted his glass, drank, and looked up in dismay. He set down his glass and flushed heavily. He was breathing hard. I watched the wife of the Ambassador, *hard,* at the end of the table. She was making frenzied conversation with the man on her right, the Undersecretary for Foreign Affairs. Her color was very high.

There was a sudden tinkle of breaking glass. Down the table, the Afghan Minister ruefully contemplated the shards of his wine goblet.

"*Dommage!*" he muttered. He bowed low to the wife of the Ambassador who *had* to look now. The tall Afghan made a regretful *moué* toward his hostess. A footman already was scraping up the broken glass and a new goblet—they were exquisite pieces—had been set in place before the Afghan Minister. His wine was poured. He lifted his glass and drank, smiled, and his twinkling eyes met mine over the rim of his uplifted goblet. It was obvious he was now drinking the *Château Margeau '34* which had been poured for most of the rest of us, including the *New York Times.*

Absolutely nothing was said after dinner about the incident. The Ambassador's wife, however, was dreadfully ill at ease—

even more so, for she paled, when toward the end of the evening the Afghan reminded the Ambassador that he had an appointment at his residence on the morrow.

A valued friend of long standing, the butler at the embassy residence almost but not quite refused my handful of notes in the currency of the local realm for a brief report on what transpired next day.

" '*Straordinary*, Sir!" he told me almost breathlessly, when he met me in a local tavern late the following evening. "Her ladyship—" all ambassadors' wives are ladyships to all butlers, "was simply *livid*, Sir. Those wineglasses are 'orribly expensive, Sir. Well, Sir, her ladyship apparently had determined to settle the score with the Afghan Minister, Sir." The butler looked down, shamefacedly. "I was just off the pantry when she was telling Ismail, the footman, to take in the brandy this afternoon, Sir. She *forced* Ismail to take in the *domestic* cognac—" The butler was enjoying his story.

"So the Afghan Minister pours himself a double hooker, Sir—I just *happened* to be tidying up off the study, you see, and I couldn't really 'elp seeing, Sir." I nodded.

"Well, Sir, the dark gentleman had a large mouthful of this filthy—pardon me, Sir—this orful local brandy, and, what do you think he did, Sir?" The embassy butler paused dramatically and exploded.

"He bloody well spewed it right out all over her ladyship's precious carpet! Spit it out, he did, *all over!* Then he says, '*Thunder!*' or something like that, Sir, and poor Ismail stood there trembling, and the Afghan Minister gave him what's for in French. It was *something*, Sir—it was a caution!" The butler paused dramatically, breathing hard, and went on.

"Well, Sir, the Ambassador himself was just coming in. He shouted for Ismail to get out—and I've never seen His Excellency so angry, Sir—and he rang the bell for me, Sir. I went in straightway with an uncorked bottle of Armagnac and I opened it right there." He spread his palms on the tile-topped table.

"And you know what, Sir? Her ladyship was havin' hysterics upstairs, Sir, about what she called her precious Bok-, er, Bok-arry carpet—"

"Bokhara," I suggested.

"Yes, Sir. About the carpet. And you could hear her all over the residence, but the maid told me about her carrying on so." The butler looked nervously over his shoulder.

"You know what else, Sir?" he said. "When I left tonight, just a few minutes ago, her ladyship was still upstairs—but the Afghan gentleman and His Excellency, the Ambassador, was still sittin' in the study, Sir, with the *second* bottle of the Armagnac I brought 'em, and laughing, Sir, fit to kill!"

The foregoing story is exclusive in its detail, but the story itself is widely known. So, unhappily, were all the principals involved, and the Western arrogance which precipitated it.

New wine in old bottles is as nauseatingly unacceptable to the proud Afghans as to most of the peoples of mid-Asia and the Middle East. There are exceptions, among these exceptional people, but only a few.

Baksheesh! is the perennial cry of the beggar children in the bazaars of Syria and the streets of Amman in Jordan; from the malformed, diseased supplicants in the Cairo alleyways, and the slinking beggar-women of Khartoum, Benghazi, Tangiers, Algiers and Casablanca. Earlier, the writer sought to point out that the handful of piastres one hands a Cairo beggar usually are received in the classic tradition: the beggar spits over his left shoulder and mutters an incantation against the unwelcome Western infidel. So with the crisp green packets of American dollars handed to venal Moslem middlemen—the slave-driving local contractors on the innumerable and vast manual labor jobs, from Middle Eastern airports and roadways to sewage systems; with the myriad governmental officials who let these selfsame contracts for American money safely paid to dummy accounts in Switzerland and American banks (most of them, oddly, in Brooklyn); with stevedore organizers in the ports of Istanbul, Greece's Piraeus, Beirut, Alexandria, Port Said, Suez and elsewhere, who make the United States waterfront "shape-up" graft look like relative chicken feed; with the thousand-and-one slick but hardened leechers of the Levant and the entire Middle East who fasten onto Point Four projects before the ink is hardly dry in Washington; with the get-rich-quick scum of American ne'er-do-wells which slimes over a portion of almost every major engineering project in the Middle East and around its vast periphery today. What incantation the Americans mutter is a mystery.

As faraway, high and mistily obscure as they may seem to Westerners, the lofty peaks of the Hindu Kush in Afghanistan might be an ideal vantage from which the West could take a figurative *shufti*—a look-see—backward across the embroiling lands and peoples of the Middle East and the areas around the Middle Eastern frontiers.

Disillusionment with the West is abysmally profound in nearly all of the Middle East. Communist dialectics is largely mumbo jumbo to Islam's millions, but no such dogma is being preached, sold and smuggled to the teeming millions of Arab and Moslem peoples. On the contrary, they are being sold, and very successfully, upon a policy of mistrust and hatred and contempt directed toward the West, and simultaneously are being injected with the deadly virus of wild, hopeless "nationalism" which already has stricken Iran and may overwhelm Egypt and other Middle Eastern states before 1952 is half gone.

Western policy is dismally divided between a kind of police action and the role of a jittery but determined young social worker who is laden with platitudes, a few goodies and an inexorable financial form which wants to know what the family income was last month.

Join us! entreats the West, and we will help you to defeat Communism, hunger, disease and poverty, the chinch bug, the man-eating shark, the housefly and, in time, the common cold. *See*—here are some beautiful American dollars and a lot of blueprints to prove it.

Join us! says Soviet Russia, and here is a rifle. Kill your despotic rulers. Throw out the infidels from the West. Take freedom in your hands! Somewhere between a phony battle cry and a shameful litany, it is harsh, strident, but amazingly melodic to ears unattuned to Western counterpoint.

Like the bells on the pigeons of mythical Shangri-La, the Soviet siren song sounds mystically sweet in many an Islamic ear. The wish-deed of Arabic philosophy is very nearly attuned. And the ready rifle, the handgun, the bomb, all these are tangibles.

The disputed Anglo-Egyptian Sudan, Libya, Tunisia, Algeria and Morocco seem as fantastically far away to many an Afghan as those same areas seem to many Westerners. Yet the Middle East is timeless and distances telescope in the twinkling of a political wink, whether from Washington, London, or, more often, from Moscow. In rounding out the overall picture of the Middle East and the enormous circumfer-

[204]

ence of the peoples and lands about it, the author in the next
few thousand words will attempt to bring the whole into sharp
focus. It is a challenging task, but then so was all the foregoing.

22

THE IMMENSE MOSAIC of the mighty Middle East, stained deep with the blood of centuries of warring peoples and crosshatched with endless intrigue, resembles nothing so much as a baffling picture puzzle, with some mischievous malefactor constantly stealing the pieces.

Logically, for instance, the huge, irregularly shaped puzzle-piece of the Anglo-Egyptian Sudan should be placed just south of Egypt with the Red Sea on the east, Eritrea and Ethiopia to the southeast; the Uganda Protectorate and Belgian Congo to the south, and French Equatorial Africa on the west. Geographically, of course, that is the Sudan's location, and politically the Sudan is seemingly an inseparable part of the Anglo-Egyptian crisis.

Illogically but more accurately, the Anglo-Egyptian Sudan gradually is becoming a segment of the North African Moslem struggle for independence and thus fits more snugly into the political picture with newly sovereign Libya, restive Tunisia, Algeria and Morocco. It is a difficult lesson, but the world, and particularly the West, is learning that it is not only frustrating but downright dangerous to play with even the smallest countries as if they were jigsawed pieces of a parlor game.

Elemental, no doubt, but the Anglo-Egyptian Sudan is a case in point. The Sudan covers 967,500 square miles and has about 8,000,000 people. This is an area one-quarter the size of Continental Europe and a population larger than Sweden's. It bestrides the confluence of the White and Blue Niles at Khartoum, and has become infected with the fever of nationalism which is sweeping the Middle East and Asia. While Cairo dismally ululates over the fate of the Sudanese and British colonials shed crocodile tears for these people, the Sudanese themselves want nothing so much as *out*. Out, that is, from under the shackling confines of condominium status —foreign rule by joint Anglo-Egyptian power—and an opportunity to exploit their own not inconsiderable agricultural and mineral wealth and the riches of the Nile.

The Sudanese are fierce and first-rate fighting men as they have bloodily demonstrated in the not-too-recent past. Because a major conflict anywhere else in the vast Middle East unquestionably will unleash latent revolution in the Sudan, many a Middle Eastern observer currently is reviewing not only recent but more distant history to come at a reasonably sharp focus on the future.

From earliest recorded history to the Egyptian conquest the valley of the White Nile, which flows south to north across the Sudan and loops a giant figure S to enter Egypt, and the Blue Nile, flowing downward from Eritrea, were the scenes of unremitting struggle and slaughter. Egypt brought disease, tax collectors and slavery and oppression almost unheard of even in the jungles. The advent of Gordon and Baker—Sir Samuel Baker and Colonel C. G. Gordon—heroes of the Sudan in British annals, brought only brief respite from Egyptian rapine and slaughter. With their departure, Egyptian venality, extortion and the slave traffic reappeared and intensified.

A lusty Dongolese tribesman named Mohammed Ahmed suddenly proclaimed himself the *Mahdi*, or "guide," of Islam and called for revolt. In January 1884 the Mahdi's hordes of fierce tribesmen overwhelmed and annihilated 10,000 men led by Hicks Pasha—Colonel William Hicks, who sought high adventure and found it for a while before death—and the Mahdist forces rolled on to wipe out 4,000 Egyptians and spread wild fanaticism throughout the Sudan. Now the British acted. The famous Gordon was redispatched, but too late. Mahdism was sweeping like a veldt fire throughout the land and the savage dervishes had risen to lay siege to Berber, then Khartoum. And now began the saga familiar to almost every English schoolchild, but only vaguely familiar to most adult Americans. The redoubtable General Gordon defended Khartoum from May through the blazing summer and into the fall and winter while the British Empire awaited every dispatch from the bloody Sudan with breathless expectation. Gordon secretly dispatched messengers down the Nile for help, but the mission was decoyed ashore and all murdered. A relief column started up the Nile from Cairo to save Gordon and Khartoum. It came too late. On one of the darkest days in British Imperial history, Khartoum fell by storm to the screaming Mahdist warriors on January 25, 1885, and the gallant Gordon was slain. The *Mahdi* was at the zenith of his power and monarch of the Sudan when he suddenly fell ill and died.

The Khalifa Abdullah succeeded Mohammed and ruled, during the *Mahdia* regime, until September 2, 1898, when the mighty Kitchener (later Lord Kitchener of Khartoum) led an overwhelming Anglo-Egyptian army which toppled the Khalifa and led to the eventual defeat of the entire Mahdia. Other Mahdist leaders were summarily hanged. No few hundred words can suffice for the coverage of this all-important period in Sudanese, British and Egyptian history, but the foregoing paragraphs may help shed light on what followed and what, today, may be coming.

Claiming "right of conquest," the British Government forced the condominium of joint Anglo-Egyptian rule upon the Sudanese. It was signed in September 1899. Control of the Upper Nile was established. Lord Kitchener, the first sirdar of the Sudan, left his governor-generalship a year later to sail home to a hero's welcome. His successors were benevolent, intelligent officers who brought the Sudan to slow but eventual peace and comparative prosperity such as it had never known. Taxes were light and rule was gentle. Sir Eldon Ghorst, the High Commissioner of Egypt, wrote of the Sudan in 1909 that "I do not suppose that there is any part of the world in which the mass of the population have fewer unsatisfied wants."

In the strictest sense, Sir Eldon might have been right and there are indications that the Sudanese lived for a time in peace and relative complacence. When disastrous floods brought famine in 1913, the British rushed corn from India, and old Middle Eastern hands say this was primarily responsible for the relative quiescence of the Sudan during the years of World War I.

Rule over the Sudan might have been good, but it was still foreign and there were Sudanese who had not forgotten days of independence under the corrupt but Sudanese Mahdi. Egyptian nationalists were almost as ill-advised then as today, for they sent agitators up the Nile to stir up trouble against the British. Trouble came, but it reacted violently against the Egyptians as well. In ensuing insurrections, Egyptian-inspired, the British struck back hard and the eventual result was virtual single-handed British control of the Sudan. Lonely but dutiful British officers, agents and district commissioners went about their work until, characteristically, they were speared, shot, stabbed, bombed or stoned to death by street mobs, after which His Majesty's Government usually managed to find and execute the assassins. In a word, the situation ticked along at a reasonable norm for the Middle East.

Until the late summer of 1951, aside from sporadic incidents here and there, the Anglo-Egyptian Sudan's post-World War II history was relatively quiet. It was again Egyptian fanaticism and nationalism which aroused the Sudanese to demonstrations which caused the British to beef up their garrisons in the Sudan and alert troops in nearby British Middle Eastern bivouacs. Agitation began for an enlargement of the 1948 Sudanese constitution, which enabled debate in an appointive Anglo-Sudanese executive council and approved a legislative assembly, partly elective.

Certainly it is not the outraged ghost of an almost vanished British imperialism which keeps the British garrisons at extraordinary strength and on the *qui vive* in the Sudan today. Nor could anybody but the most unreasoning Egyptian nationalist claim that the British are less popular in the Sudan than the Egyptians, and that the Sudanese should recognize King Farouk's self-appointive role as monarch of the Sudan. By the same token, it would be a grave mistake to underestimate the British temper at the moment, vis-à-vis the Sudan, and British accomplishments there.

It would be just as serious to ignore the very real nationalistic aspirations of the Sudanese, for while the heat of feeling is rising among those peoples it is the considered opinion among reliable and conscientious correspondents that this virus is relatively mild and untainted by the deadly type which is virtually epidemic almost everywhere else in Middle East. For one thing, the Sudan is the fallowest ground of all for Communist infiltration. For another, while the Sudan population is predominantly Moslem, it is neither devoutly nor fanatically susceptible to the brand of Islamic xenophobia being peddled by the Haj Amin el Husseini from his lair in Cairo. Indeed, the former Mufti has given the Sudan a wide berth in recent years. Finally, the better-educated Sudanese are genuinely appreciative of the generally benevolent rule of the British and the irrigation projects, such as the gigantic Gezira scheme, and grudgingly aware that Egypt would dry up like a cinder if she were denied the precious waters of the Niles.

Irrigation projects, land reforms, trade balances and commercial treaties are mere words to the Arabs and Negroes of the Sudan, and amazingly academic terms to many peoples many places whose very lives depend upon water, soil, imports and exports, and the uninterrupted receipt of enough currency, gold or barter to live from day to day.

Still, the Sudanese want their liberty. Their insistent demands are not even based upon a calculated risk, as in the Iranian uprisings, the Egyptian turmoil, the nationalist stirrings in Iraq and the Moslem uneasiness in Syria and the grumblings and demonstrations in Tunisia, Algeria and Morocco.

Of all the millions of restive peoples in the entire Middle East, the Sudanese are the least vital in themselves and in their current assets, and seemingly in their strategic location, to the gigantic power struggle which rages about them. Virtually isolated by the vast Libyan and Nubian deserts and the wastelands and jungle of the Uganda, the Belgian Congo and French Equatorial Africa, with one negligible water outlet, Port Sudan, on the Red Sea, and landlocked on the southeast and south by the wild uplands frontiers of Eritrea and Ethiopia, the Sudanese boast no oil, no rail or road network, nor any major bases within striking distance of potentially hostile frontiers.

Yet a large portion of the best troops the British can muster are encamped on Sudanese soil, an open invitation to an anti-British aggressor to strike at the Sudan. Why?

The question is neither academic nor captious, merely Sudanese.

If the writer has seemed unnecessarily discursive in the foregoing examination of the Sudan and the Anglo-Egyptian-Sudanese problem, it is largely because this huge northeast African country offers the least complex example, from the viewpoint of arms and man power, of Great Power intrusion upon a virtually defenseless small one. This does not exclude the example of the Red Chinese invasion of Tibet, for Tibetan bases can and probably will be implemented in any major Communist push into India, Nepal, Kashmir, Pakistan or Afghanistan.

Sudan's offensive position is negligible in all directions, with the possible exception of Egypt, and the Sudanese armed forces are small and British-controlled. Bush warfare and desert raiding, effective in the days of Kitchener, have been outmoded by the warplane and modern automatic weapons. And it would take the most extreme provocation to send the Sudanese into war against neighboring Egypt. Nor, according to this writer's information, is there the remotest chance that the Sudanese ever would, uncoerced, form any alliance with or permit annexation by Egypt.

Small wonder, under all these foregoing circumstances, that the Sudan looks with bewilderment and envy toward neighboring Libya. This giant North African country, a former Italian colony, and certainly one of the poorest and most backward in the world, received its independence in January 1952.

Poverty-ridden, defenseless, diseased and 90 per cent illiterate in its population of 1,072,000 Arabs, Libya was as unprepared for statehood as the veriest desert rabble. Under approval of the United Nations General Assembly, however, the 680,000 miles of almost barren desert reached full independence. Libya, moreover, becomes an immediate financial liability upon Great Britain which must meet Libya's annual budget deficit of nearly a half million dollars, and dispatch paid foreign advisers to begin the long, painful and probably hopeless effort to pull this desert kingdom out of the red and into something resembling genuine autonomy.

Libya's monarch is burnoosed King Idris I, formerly the Emir of Cyrenaica, one of Libya's three major desert provinces, and he has a dreary outlook ahead. Annual per capita income in Libya is roughly $30 per head and the Libyan economy could be upset by almost any internal disturbances or trouble on Libya's frontiers with Egypt, the Anglo-Egyptian Sudan, French Equatorial Africa, French West Africa, Algeria or Tunisia. Such troubles, internal and external, may not be long in coming. King Idris' political opposition is vested in a powerful and rabidly anti-Western desert coalition party headed by Beshir Bey Sadawi, a hard-riding part-time bandit who has a reputedly desperate following of nomadic bullies.

The *why* of Libyan independence at this time can be answered only by the usual Western reasons offered up for the presence of British occupation forces in the Sudan and along the Suez Canal, in Iraq and on Cyprus and Malta, and by the frenzied building of giant American air bases throughout the Middle East, and the presence of the U. S. Sixth Fleet and major units of the British fleet in the eastern Mediterranean, namely: Security.

Libya's strategic position almost midway upon the Mediterranean coast of North Africa has made it a prize of rival dynastic opportunists since before the birth of Christ. Carthage seized it first, to be followed by the Romans, the Vandals, the rampaging Islamic conquerors, the Ottoman Empire and finally Italy, which received this strategic but untidy and uneconomical reward in 1911. Italy did very little for her new colony and its miserable peoples subsisted, as they had done for centuries, on dates, olives, lemons and banditry against camel caravans in the desert. The advent of Mussolini and the Duce's vaulting ambitions gave birth to the abortive plan to unload Italy's disproportionately high population upon Libyan soil in a vast emigration. The first boatloads hardly had been landed on this bleak North African shore before they were screaming to be taken off again.

Libya's helpless, passive role in World War II is a shoddy, bloody history known to Americans through the headlines reporting the battledore-and-shuttlecock coastwise campaigning of the Italians, and later the *Afrikakorps*, against the tireless, gallant and indomitable "Desert Rats" of the British Eighth Army. Benghazi also was the secret take-off point for the murderously costly low-level raids against Romania's Ploesti oilfields and refineries by the U. S. Eighth Air Force's B-24's.

Libyan military history, so repetitious, is underscored by the presence near Tripoli today of giant Wheelus Field, a

[214]

USAFSAC base, a million-dollar installation designed specifically for the atomic bombing of innermost Russian bases by the longest-range bombers in the Strategic Air Command. Wheelus' runways are just 1,960 airline miles from the crenelated towers of the Kremlin.

The United States, Britain and France will advance Libya some $10,000,000 during 1952 to assist this gigantic land-poor desert kingdom toward subsistence. All of which is splendid for Libya and the Allied security program in the Middle East.

However, the repercussions from Libyan independence are creating whorls of political turbulence upon political seismographs from one end of the Middle East to the other, and beyond. Neighboring Tunisia and her sister French protectorates, Algeria and Morocco, have been goaded into fresh howls of anguish. Egypt is intensely irritated, for Egyptian efforts to capture Libyan leadership were blatantly open and futile. And Egypt realizes that the Sudan cannot view Libya's new freedom with equanimity. The Sudanese are one more large stride removed from any cadence with the Egyptians, who were badly out of step anyway.

The new kingdom in Libya has further unsettled the unsteady, simmering Middle East, shaking up and lighting bonfires under the intransigent Arabs, and the large, well-to-do and extremely vocal European *émigré* populations in Tunis, Algiers and Morocco; and, unavoidably, calling direct attention to businesslike Allied preparations for all-out war when it comes to this fear-ridden part of the world.

France had until recently ridden out the gales of native discontent in its Middle East protectorates while fighting a bloody, costly defensive campaign in Indo-China. The danger signals are now posted for France, and perhaps for her Allies, along the sandy, battle-scarred littoral of Northwest Africa.

23

STRATEGIC NORTHWEST AFRICA rims the turbulent Middle East at its western extremity even as faraway Pakistan, wedged deep in the middle of Asia, stands at the easternmost flank of this selfsame vital theatre of potential war. Such geographical enigmas are perplexing and even infuriating to some Western thinking, as baffling as the stubborn political fact that Pakistan has been the foremost champion of Tunisian independence.

How explain it, this telescoping of geography and enormous distances? How rationalize concerted, serious and sincere political action by a French protectorate on the Mediterranean and an Asiatic Power almost half a world away? The oversimplified answer is that the Mercator projection in map-making is as out-dated as much current political thinking—flat, unrealistic and stalely dangerous. (The author hastens to add that the Mercator treatment of the maps in the end-papers of

Blood, Oil and Sand is due to limitations of space, pointing out
that the charts *are* curvilinear.)

The rumblings of discontent in Tunisia and Morocco are no
less deep-seated than the volcanic political tremors in the
Middle Eastern heartland. The fact that the Iranian and
Egyptian outbursts are fanatical and essentially immoral does
not mean that national independence is *ipso facto* bad, or that
the burning motives behind agitation for freedom are always
sordid, foolish or both.

Tunisia is tired, after seventy-one years of French domination. Morocco is weary of French and Spanish rule and chafing
for independence. Algeria is nominally a part of France
proper, but members of its largely indigenous population do
not enjoy the full political privileges of metropolitan Frenchmen. Tunisia's demands are the loudest, the best phrased and
on the whole the most meritorious, but the West cannot long
ignore Algerian unrest and Moroccan choler, for all three
French territories are inextricably bound up with Allied security, and indeed, the United States is laying five of its largest and most precious eggs, giant airdomes, squarely in the
tricky Moroccan basket.

Tunis, Algeria and Morocco actually are but artificial political divisions of one huge natural area, old Barbary, which
to one degree or another was dominated, Tunisia in particular,
by the ruthless Turks of the Ottoman Empire. The populations
are Arabic and Berber, Berberized Arabs or Arabized Berbers,
with a large late-coming European population which has lent
strength and cunning political direction to native demands for
sovereignty. Although the two races have intermingled
through the centuries, there are still important anthropological differences which reflect themselves very importantly in
the everyday life of these peoples.

Briefly, the Berbers are generally light-skinned and in many cases, blond, although the winds and desert suns burn the Berbers to a swarthiness matching the natural pigmentation of real Arabs. By temperament there are several marked differences, all important. The Berbers are essentially farmers with a passionate love of the soil. Fighters and brigands, too, they nevertheless revere social order and local rulers usually are elected by tribal leaders. There are complicated intertribal political relations, especially in time of war, and none of the wild, hell-for-leather anarchy which marks the Arabs. Berbers are excellent craftsmen and it is their silverwork, carpets, pottery and leather goods which early attracted trade to Northwest Africa. Berber medicine is still largely witchcraft, but with some startling exceptions in the use of some desert-grown herbs, and primitive surgery has made extraordinary strides, including sterile amputations, bone grafting and even brain trephining.

Arabic traits are familiar across millions of square miles of Africa and the Middle East. Haughty and arrogant, the Arabs consider themselves an aristocracy and behave accordingly. Tribal rule is by inheritance and tribal revolt usually is directed against an individual or a tribe, rather than a system. While there is an understandable contempt among these people, one for the other, they have nevertheless intermarried and allied themselves in desert warfare until, in some areas, especially in Algiers itself and Morocco, no stranger can distinguish between them.

Tunis and Tunisia have achieved a high degree of capability for self-government, thanks largely to Berber industry and ingenuity and to relatively benevolent French rule. Tunisia's 48,000 square miles on the North African coast, spearing outward at Cap Bon toward Sicily, numbers a population of some 3,200,000, including more than 125,000 aliens. Nearly all of these people are increasingly restive, especially since the U.N. grant of independence to neighboring Libya, and Habib Bourguiba, the able president of the powerful Neodestour Independence party, is agitating unceasingly at home and abroad, notably through U.N. lobbies, for recognition of Tunisia's grievances.

France has ruled Tunisia since 1881 when a serious rising of the Khroumer tribes brought invading French forces to crush the revolt. The French established a protectorate and have maintained it ever since, with increasing degrees of leniency and extensions of self-government to the Arab and Bedouin leaders. Tunisians protest this is not enough and point to Tunisia's demonstrated ability to maintain itself upon its lush agriculture and large exports of olive oil, minerals, grains and fruits. Premier Mohammed Chenik in 1950–51 summoned Arab statesmen from ten countries and prepared to confront France and the U.N. with a solid Moslem front supporting Tunisian autonomy. Anglo-French diplomacy, with a certain amount of aid from the United States, managed to crack the united front, when many of the Arab leaders begged off with the plea that they were too involved in similar problems within their own states. The Pakistanis stood fast with the Tunisians. Tunisian resistance was sufficient to force France to dispatch a new Resident General, and in the spring of 1951 Tunisian nationalists were threatening a continuation of general strikes, demonstrations, boycotts of French goods and other strong measures to speed the French to a recognition of Tunisian independence.

Algerian intransigence is vastly more moderate than the marshaled, urgent and businesslike agitation of Tunisia and, in consequence, falls upon more sympathetic ears in the mother country. This bloody, sandy French protectorate was the scene, with Tunisia, of some of the heaviest of the early American fighting in World War II as the invading U. S. forces drove eastward to chew up the deadly *Afrikakorps*. Algiers itself and its vastly overrated Casbah are known to scores of thousands of American GI's and officers who flowed through the great port en route to Sicily, southern France and the Italian boot. Algeria is bounded, of course, by Tunisia on the east and Morocco on the west and beyond, some 350 miles into the desert, by the limitless Sahara. Algeria numbers a population of some 8,600,000 Moslems, Arabs, Bedouins and Berbers, and the city of Algiers itself has a large European population among its teeming thousands. European capital and know-how have taken over most of the fertile Tell area on the coast, which is being cultivated scientifically and profitably. Inland and upward in the Atlas mountains, cattle grazing is the most lucrative pursuit, although American and European enterprises are exploring mining projects in iron, lead, zinc, copper and antimony.

In the Army code, however, Tunisia, Algeria and Morocco are strictly *bases, Allied, military, for the use of*, and the Point Four aid to Libya and ECA (now Mutual Security Administration) assistance to Algeria and Morocco are strictly security measures. The myriad peoples are plainly, sometimes contemptuously, aware of it. Like a rather unattractive girl who has somehow wrangled her first prom, the peoples of this area are thoroughly familiar with the sudden rush of attention on special occasions, and the sudden rush away of the suitors when the need is gone.

The need is there again, and so are the ready American dollars, the food and the shiploads of machinery and motor transport, the engineers and the Army, and the bombers. There is also the renewed beneficence of the ruling French, but not, in the opinion of the natives, enough of it. Not nearly. Moroccan nationalists know the real depth of American need for their country and this time they are staking their admission price tags firmly in the soil, and prominently for all to see.

Historic Morocco undoubtedly will be the central theatre in the final showdown between the insistent, increasingly violent Arab and Berber Moslem nationalists, the reluctant French and the well-meaning, well-heeled but naive Americans in Northwest Africa.

The valid reasons are fairly simple to come at.

Morocco was deliberately chosen as the safest, most strategic site for the largest groupment of giant American air bases aimed at Russia—the biggest overseas military project since World War II—and the Moroccans know it.

French intercession was needed, in actuality, to secure permission from the Sultan of Morocco to construct the bases. True, the French could have ignored the Sultan and unilaterally given their approval, but such action almost undoubtedly would have inspired far more serious incidents than the November 1951 riots at Casablanca, possibly even nation-wide revolt. And the Moroccans know it.

Moroccan nationalist pressure immediately was exerted to force the State Department to urge the French Government toward a speed-up in self-government for Morocco. All Moroccans knew it, for leaders of the powerful Istiqlal (nationalist) party circulated the word even as the first shiploads of American equipment arrived.

Franco-American policy cleavages then would become inevitable, and the Moroccans knew it. The entire Moslem world knew it, and the Arab League bloc aided by India ganged up on State Department aides and American delegates to the

U.N. to insure that they would not forget it. Moroccans are long used to duplicity and the trick delays of diplomacy, and Moroccan leaders sharply reminded our representatives of this salient fact. Our policy makers also were reminded of an apocryphal story: that the late President Roosevelt as early as the celebrated Casablanca conference firmly promised the Sultan of Morocco that Moroccan liberation ultimately was assured under American sanction. There is no record of such a promise, although the Sultan did consult with the President, but it is an unshakable legend in all Morocco and, aided by the mystic Arabic wish-deed philosophy, it is an absolute fact—to Moroccans.

General Augustin Guillaume, the French Resident General in Morocco, sought repeatedly through the late winter of 1951–52 to disabuse the Moroccan leaders of the belief that the presence of Americans insured their imminent independence. French logic is traditionally worse than useless against Islamic mysticism. The Moroccans believe what they believe.

The U. S. bomber bases, meantime, are nearing completion with long runways sufficient to handle the longest-ranged U. S. bombers, even those still on the drawing boards. By midsummer of 1952, most of the Moroccan installations will be complete. To the Army and Air Force that is enough. Unhappily, for American diplomats who must now face the Franco-Moroccan showdown, this is only the beginning.

The roiling monarchy of Morocco contains far more than the sperm of isolated and sporadic violence and revolt. Spawned during the political *mésalliances* which followed the breakup of the giant Shereefian Empire which had existed from the seventh century, modern Morocco is peopled predominantly by descendants of the fierce Berbers who ravaged Spain three times. These selfsame descendants aided in the

[222]

fourth ravagement from Spanish Morocco in the course of the Spanish Civil War of 1936–39 when the savage Moors or Moros—Arab-Berber warriors—spearheaded the Fascist invasion of Republican Spain led by the Fascist General, Sanjurjo, whose mysterious death in a plane crash upped Francisco Franco from obscurity to his present dizzy eminence. The aboriginal Berbers of present-day Morocco have demonstrated that they are as dangerous, when armed and trained, as their forebears.

As presently constituted, Morocco is a theoretical absolute monarchy under the Sultan, who makes Rabat his residence, although Fez, Marrakech and Meknes are also spiritual capitals; but the country is, of course, ruled by France, with minor Spanish assistance. The entire monarchy covers some 172,000 square miles, with a population of about 9,600,000. The hills of the Rif border the Mediterranean littoral and the Grand Atlas mountains rise behind them in a northeast-southwest series of five ranges which tower to 12,000 feet or more. It was the slippery Abd-el-Krim who came out of the Rif to lead the last of the twenty-year-long campaigns against French invasion and occupancy of Algeria and Morocco.

Neutral Tangier is an international settlement on the spur of Spanish Morocco beyond the western passage of the Strait of Gibraltar. Tangier Zone has some 100,000 inhabitants, 60,000 of whom inhabit the city. About 3,000 of these are engaged in every manner of nefarious trade in drugs, women, "black" commodities and, of course, money. The police, under a 1928 ruling, were Spanish and amiable, until it was established that they had been *too* amiable in the way of profit sharing; the police, with the Spanish Fascist militia who had occupied Tangier in 1940, were tossed out. The present international police are still in the good graces of the black market and drug ring which virtually controls Tangier, a kind of western Hong Kong.

Spain perhaps mischievously early in 1952 extended amnesty to a number of Arab nationalist leaders who had fled Spanish Morocco, and at the same time promised greater autonomy to Spanish Arabs. This roiled even deeper the feelings of French Arabs just over the frontier. Franco-Spanish relations consequently were ruffled again. Adding to the general confusion of the entire picture is the fact that nearly two million French and other European settlers have made their homes in the Moroccan and Tunisian protectorates and in Algeria, amassed considerable wealth with Western methods, and are themselves demanding a hand in government.

But—*bases.* While it is well to keep in mind and in well-polished condition the multifarious issues dividing and subdividing the peoples and lands of the strategic Northwest African coastal areas and the interior, the overriding concern of the Great Powers of the West is to prevent neutrality or enemy occupation here in the event of the expected war with Russia. To this end, even the native rulers and police have turned a ready hand, for Communism is unpopular and its spurious export license of "nationalism," which has been accepted in large areas of the less politically sophisticated Middle East, is coldly rejected by the Moroccan Berbers and Arabs.

On the contrary, Moroccan leaders charge, with some accuracy, that Communism has been strictly a French import. The Communist colony in Tangier, Ceuta and Tetuan in Spanish Morocco, Rabat, Meknes, Fez and Marrakech is estimated at some 2,500 to 3,000 underpaid quislings whose main job it is to spy on the new American installations. Tangier is the pay-off point and sanctuary for Red agents, but, aside from occasional legitimate and reliable information Soviet operatives may secure about forthcoming Moroccan nationalist maneuvers, it would seem that the Kremlin is wasting its dollar supply on intelligence exposing American installations in Northwest Africa.

While it is true that such conditions change from month to month, week to week and almost day to day, American intelligence security in Northwest Africa is approximately on par with the same mercurial product throughout the Middle East: approximately nil. If the strength and length of the runways at Wheelus Field, Libya, and on the new airdromes in Morocco are a puzzle to Soviet agents, then such agents need the services of a phrenologist and psychiatrist. The location of ammo and bomb dumps, fuel dumps and flak installations, power lines and depots, assembly and repair shacks, motor pools and the BOQ's (Bachelors' Officers Quarters) are as transparently protected by security as the latrines. Unhappily, the same situation prevails throughout most of the Middle East and its periphery. Were the obvious and readily approachable facts unavailable, the enemy agent has only to frequent the nearest *boîte* or *bistro* to hear the never-ending scuttlebutt, the gripes and the beefs and the groanings of the engineers and the construction "stiffs" who spend their off-time with virtually the only available solace, the local alkys—*raki, arak, douziko,* raw wine or vodka. Arab or Berber women are *tabu* to any man but a maniac. The venereal rate in all the Middle East is horrendous, but in Morocco, Algiers and Libya, as in areas of the Sudan, at Port Said, Suez, throughout the Persian Gulf and in Iraq there are VD maladies which, until World War II, had never even been heard of, and which still defy analysis.

The "slow-boat"-home treatment for working stiffs, consultants, engineers and even laboratory technicians among the enormous crews of Americans sent overseas on defense work is staggering. The oil industry has its large, but diminishing spate, too, for Stateside screening for high-paid jobs with petroleum companies is getting stiffer. And the term itself actually is a misnomer. Even the $200-$250-per-week American laborer with overseas defense projects puts away enough money within a few weeks to finance a flight home when the high-paying job in "romantic" Casablanca fails to pan out as expected. Or Rabat. Or Boulhaut. Or Nouasseur. Or Ben Guerir, deep in the Moroccan desert. Or Wheelus in Libya, Dhahran in Saudi Arabia, the faraway and genuinely isolated posts in the Turkish hinterlands, or almost numberless other posts on the 150-odd major American air installations scattered about in the Middle East, Asia, on the ice-caps, or elsewhere.

Homesickness, boredom, sex hunger and incipient alcoholism account for most "war defense" casualties overseas, in that order.

The rate, however, is highest in the Middle East and environs.

The American weaknesses are accepted here with candor, dispassionate understanding, and only rarely contempt, even when the "D & D" (drunk and disorderly) rate hits 90 per cent of arrests in Casablanca.

The foregoing side glance into one of the more sordid offshoots of Western, and almost specifically American, avenues of defense is a minuscule candid shot of the huge and generally reassuring picture. Politically, the West is still dreadfully out of sync in most of the thirty-seven nations that the United States is treaty-bound to defend in case of foreign aggression, and the additional ten or twelve countries and colonies to which we are committed by the presence of American troops or by mutual understandings. Militarily, despite administrational mistakes beyond recall and a horde of hampering miscalculations which have squeezed down the delivery of arms and equipment to vital Allied countries, the mosaic is not so dark.

It is dark enough, however.

The outer perimeter of the boiling, sanguinary and reckless Middle East is also deep in shadow.

The peoples and the countries of the Middle East are wracked by all these seemingly insoluble problems, and by the inexorable, crushing pressure of the Soviets and the powerful but dissipated and divided strength of the West.

Something has to give or burst.

24

IMMATURITY AND BAD FAITH are stamped indelibly upon American policy in the cynical eyes and unsettled minds of the heterogeneous peoples whose very existence is at the whim of the Great Powers now constricting their encirclement of the enormous Middle East.

Postwar disillusionment has very nearly reached its depths in the hearts of teeming millions who had hoped that fumbling but benevolent American policy might succeed where British colonialism had so miserably failed. On the contrary, Moslem and Arab leaders and their inflammable massed millions of followers have become convinced that America, not Britain, and *not Communist Russia,* is the implacable enemy of their aspirations for independence, freedom from hunger, privations and pestilence and an opportunity to solve their grinding economic woes and the scourge of almost unending war.

Why?

Because catastrophic wartime and postwar mistakes in U. S.

foreign policy have denuded America today of virtually every bargaining point in the Middle East save naked force and money.

The sickening realization is being driven home to Americans that money, incredibly, is not enough to elicit the hope and faith and cooperation of inflamed peoples bred on centuries of Great Power perfidy, exploitation and arrogance; that sheer force, in the shape of terrifying bombs and bombers, battleships and aircraft carriers, jet warplanes and guided missles, tanks and small arms of fantastic firepower can coerce but cannot compel the Middle East's millions to ally themselves with the West against the common enemy, Russia.

Despite Russian aggression in both hemispheres, and in the face of Russia's unmistakable plans for imminent adventure in the vital, strategic and fabulously oil-wealthy Middle East, the peoples of that desperate and frightened area hardheadedly refuse to unite for common defense. In particular, with only two major exceptions, they flatly and defiantly refuse to unite under the mistrusted aegis of the United States and the hated and weakened leadership of Great Britain.

Unless democracy can recapture the imagination of the Middle Eastern peoples, neither America nor Britain nor their handful of allies in the Levant can hope to withstand the onslaught of implacable Communism.

A cold-blooded military appraisal of the situation can only lead to the conclusion that a Western coalition ultimately could defeat Soviet Russia and its growing, expanding satellites, but only after a ghastly war of attrition costing unimaginable millions of lives, cities and homes throughout the world. The fact that the first and foremost battlefields in this expected war lie in the Middle Eastern heartland is not lost upon the peoples who now dwell there.

Yet the vast majority of these selfsame peoples, hating the outside world and each other, clamoring for self-determination *now*, coolly profess to view with equanimity the oncoming struggle between Russia and the West, as if this hideous Armageddon were scheduled to be fought under Marquis of Queensbury rules, or in some forest glade with lances and armored white chargers, and with the traditional spirit of noble knighthood.

How explain this seeming idiocy, this ghastly political paradox? Very many, if not most, of the answers are to be found in the foregoing chapters examining and analyzing the stormy, bloody histories of the peoples of the Middle East, and the Balkans, mid-Asia and North Africa in the smoldering peripheral area about the most dangerous single land mass on earth.

It is no good ascribing this weird attitude of the Middle Eastern peoples to any mystic kind of death wish or a desire to indulge in mass suicide in *Juggernaut* rites, in which the fanatically religious faithful cast themselves beneath the wheels of a monstrous, lumbering conveyance which supports an idol representing fate. Nor is there more than a tiny shard of truth to the theory that the Moslem peoples support a wishful hope that was popular at the time of the Nazi German onslaught on Russia, with the final involvement of the United States. That wish was best expressed by the nursery rhyme about the Gingham Dog and the Calico Cat in which the combatants devoured each other completely, and that was that. The Moslem peoples of the Middle East are romantic, fanatically religious and given to dreams of fantasy. But they are not that dreamy and not that fantastic.

In their hearts, and in the minds of their leaders, the good ones and the bad, the Middle Eastern peoples are almost as dreadfully afraid of war as the peoples of the West. *Almost* as afraid, because they have known every face of war down the centuries and it is axiomatic that the known thing is less dreadful than the unknown. England knew the terror of the blitz, but the British peoples have not experienced the misery and degradation of invasion since 1066, and Britain's hit-and-run invasion of the United States was as far distant as 1812.

The miserable peoples of the Balkans and the Middle East have tasted the bitterest dregs of war and invasion in every major world conflict since the beginning of recorded time.

It would be too simple to ascribe the apparent fatalism of the Middle Eastern peoples to their outwardly calm conclusion that, in the coming conflict between Russia and the West, they have almost everything to gain and little or nothing to lose. Yet in their opinion this is true.

The livid dangers of Communism have been vividly painted to the peoples of Middle East through virtually every means at the disposal of Western propagandists. Yet the people remain unmoved. In addition, they frequently are deeply offended by the context of Western propaganda, particularly that brand offered by the Voice of America and the operatives of USIS (the United States Information Service), both of whom affect a condescension toward the Arabic peoples that is too often intolerable. American exaltation of private enterprise and the individual is well and good, for Westerners. Private enterprise, as limned by American propagandists in terms of electric refrigerators, automobile production, the questionable amours of prominent actresses and the extensive forensics of American speechmakers (especially Administration spokesmen), leaves the Arab in the hot bazaar cold. As for the American emphasis upon the rights of the individual, the Arab is one of the most anarchistic individualists in the world and he wonders dimly why Americans make such a fuss about this issue.

Bogus Russian propaganda about community welfare, bogus as it is, goes down very well in the Middle East. Russia promises pie in the sky, but pie at least is something tangible that the Moslem peoples can understand. American tractors, modern plumbing, chewing gum and soft drinks stir the Arab not at all. Anybody who has traveled on some of the more modern trains through Arab countries is aware of Arab puzzlement about our plumbing conveniences and his disdain to use them as we intended. Russian agents promise, and promptly if stealthily deliver, rifles, small arms and ammunition, bombs and explosives to various irredentists. A rifle, a pistol, a bomb, an available woman, a horse—all these the Arab peoples readily understand. Their real or fancied tormentors are close at hand. As has been repeatedly amplified in this book, political murder is commonplace in the Middle East.

Small things, most of the foregoing, but dreadfully important in the deadly game in which the Americans have involved themselves in the countries of the Middle East. A casual Middle Eastern traveler is inclined to the thought so often expressed that "The British do it better." Indeed, it sometimes seems that they do, for they have been doing it longer, and for a time successfully.

The British were learning fast when their time ran out. The fact that much of their learning—the final recognition of the Asiatic or the Moslem as an individual—came too late, is now largely academic to the British. And theoretical as this knowledge seems, it is now becoming desperately practical that Americans swarming into the Middle East should thoroughly understand it in its every shade of meaning. Now or never—

never, that is, this side of the oncoming conflict—must the West measure their new neighbors and associates as equals, as human beings, as political peers, as military allies.

How to overcome their current defiance, insolence and intransigence is the first major problem. Turkey's example has aided immeasurably already. And the conduct of the Joint Allied Military Mission to Aid Turkey has become a criterion for the measurement of the men and the munitions now being shipped or ticketed for shipment to future potential allies in the Middle East.

The purely military aspects of this problem will be dealt with in the next, concluding chapter, but American diplomacy and the implementation of Point Four and the Mutual Security Assistance program are almost as urgent. The fact that the United States finally has recognized this urgency is sharply delineated in the appointment, early in 1952, of George C. McGhee, an Assistant Secretary of State, to head the entire mission to Turkey. McGhee is young (thirty-nine), vigorous and thoroughly versed in the problems, not only of Turkey but the entire Middle East and nearby mid-Asia.

The McGhee appointment seems a step in the right direction, but it is only a step. The appointment of Edwin Locke of the Chase Bank to head up American economic aid to the Middle East is one more stride.

The next bold strides, politically and economically, should envision, and speedily encompass, a shake-up in the whole foreign service throughout the Middle East and the entire administration of aid through the Mutual Security Administration in this area. The American diplomatic corps in the Middle East is loaded with dead wood, burdened with unimaginative and uninspired foreign service hacks and tainted with left-wing sympathizers. This is specifically true of the diplomatic missions to Belgrade, Greece, Ankara, Beirut, Iraq, Syria, Teheran and Egypt.

Free enterprise or no, American military attachés in areas containing "classified" (secret) engineering projects such as the construction of military airdromes, roads, railways, port installations, meteorological surveys, storage depots, ammunition warehouses and fuel depots and other war impedimenta, *should be empowered to recommend the summary dismissal and removal of any U. S. citizen endangering security* through direct or indirect activities affecting the control of information about such operations. The action of the military attachés should be subject to review, but not control, by the United States Ambassador or Minister in each instance. The final authority should be the War Department. If such a recommendation smacks of wartime controls, it is handy to remember that the United States *is* at war in the Middle East, to all intents and purposes, and under current loose security regulations the enemy has ready access to information of the most precious character.

American foreign policy in the whole of the Middle East should be subjected to immediate review by a joint Congressional subcommittee empowered to examine specifically:

(1) The issue of Palestine, one of the most dangerous in the Middle East;

(2) American intrusion in and mishandling of the Iranian oil crisis;

(3) The open scandal of continued arms and financial disbursements to the Communist regime of Marshal Tito of Yugoslavia;

(4) Extremely sinister influences at work in connection with the "screening" and use of European émigrés to Turkey, particularly Bulgarians, who are being used in connection with

the broadcasts of Radio Free Europe (the most effective medium, thus far, of American propaganda in the Balkans and the Middle East);

(5) A prompt investigation of the USIS, which currently is sending and maintaining overseas, particularly in the Middle East, incompetent writers and editors totally unsuited to the handling of news of the United States; and in this connection;

(6) A sharp examination of the quality and content of USIS news bulletins themselves, which currently tend to reflect only the policies of the State Department and give a distorted picture of political news emanating from the United States. This is of vital importance in an election year, for all the world, and the Middle East in particular, is watching our political conventions and the elections with an intensity that probably has not been surpassed since the elections of 1940.

Like it or not, the United States is up to its ears in one of the most complicated struggles in its diplomatic, political, economic, and probably military history. The stakes are enormous, involving the winning or loss of the current cold war and the possible loss of a hot one. Again, like it or not, the best allies of the United States in the vast Middle East are "strong men," some of them corrupt and all of them subject to the internal stresses and strains of their uneasy countries, but United States policy can and must be made without regard to pressure groups, lobbies and special interests, at home and abroad. *And this includes Zionist organizations, the Arab League, oil companies, Bulgarian and Croatian irredentists, moneyed and corrupt export-import operators, and the black marketeers who infest every Middle Eastern capital and major port throughout the Levant and North Africa.*

Listen to the cry of intransigent Egypt, from the lips of a

wild mullah in Cairo—and this war cry echoes the fervent hate of millions of Moslems throughout the two million square miles of the Middle East:

"We will knock at the doors of heaven," he cried, *"with the heads of Englishmen! We must reject any treaty which will tie us to America, which created Israel; to France, which occupies North Africa; to Turkey, whose sinful past we have not forgotten; or to Britain, which has destroyed the foundations of our independence!"*

See?

It is no easy task that we in America have set ourselves, or had thrust upon us. And, unhappily, we do not have the best material in the world at our command in the diplomatic and political corps with which to deal with the dilemma.

Come what may, the United States will find itself from time to time forced to ally itself politically with the fading and hated colonial policies of Great Britain and France. This will further outrage the Middle Eastern peoples. But our future, calculated sins are a product of our thoughtless past in this critical area of the world. The sordid and makeshift American policies of wartime Yugoslavia, and the bootless, halfhearted failures of diplomacy in Hungary and Romania; protracted stalemates in Washington which very nearly cost Turkish support in the current struggle; serious errors in Greece, which failed until almost the eleventh hour to recognize the burgeoning threat of Communism in Hellas; blunderings in Iran and Iraq and miscalculations in the Lebanon and Syria; the inexcusable mishandling of the entire Palestinian issue, and thimble-rigging meddling in Egypt—all these failures and many, many more are haunting the White House and the Department of State today.

The Middle East is a raging veldt fire in which American

inaction and stupidity, occasional venality and downright pro-Communist operations have served no cause but that of the Kremlin, inflaming the Moslem peoples and the already blazing torch of Islam. Whether we can yet quench the flames of internal disorder and bring piecemeal understanding before the oncoming holocaust is still a tossup.

The odds are long against us, as are the people, presently. Immaturity and bad faith are stamped indelibly on one side of the coin. *Inshallah*—if God is willing—it will come up on the other side. It is highly unlikely that it will stand on edge.

25

THE BLOOD SPILLED by the West in defense of the oily sands of the Middle East is not the blood of altruism.

The oncoming war with Russia, overriding and engulfing the Communists' calculated "bleeding" campaigns in Asia and drowning out the world-wide psychological and economic "cold war," almost inevitably will create its vortex in the Middle East. Already caught in the beginnings of this gigantic whirlpool, the Western powers no longer can pretend paternal or fraternal interests in the peoples, oil and bases of the Middle East and fob off these peoples and their own conscience with Korean-styled "police actions"—for the West must now stand and fight in the Middle East as if its very life depended on it, which it does.

Even now it may be too late to parry Russia's first probing attacks, to roll with the punches and attempt to ride out the earlier rounds when the West will be overwhelmingly out-numbered in the vital elements of immediate manpower,

[238]

tactical aircraft, armor and supplies. Allied forces are spread desperately thin around the world. Logistics, the problem of supply, is colossal.

The Commander in Chief of Allied Forces in Southern Europe, Admiral Robert B. Carney, a vigorous fifty-seven-year-old Californian, won World War II decorations for expertness in logistics, as well as for "extraordinary heroism" in the Pacific fighting. Carney's first task—with that of Vice Admiral Matthias B. Gardner, Commander of the Sixth Fleet, USN, the Mediterranean—will be the immediate defense of the Middle East and the Mediterranean when Russia strikes. This correspondent, on the last leg of a 23,000-mile journey through the Middle East and the Mediterranean, covered the headquarters commands of the Southern European staff chief and the Sixth Fleet at Naples. Nothing that has transpired in the brief interim since that coverage has altered the picture. On the contrary, it is in sharper focus than ever. Here, then, in the following paragraphs, is a summation of the Allied defensive mosaic, in thinking, in strategy and tactics, as drawn from Carney, Gardner, Lieutenant General William H. Arnold, Chief of JAMMAT in Turkey, and from Allied military, naval and air attachés and intelligence officers in the key areas of the Middle East and the Mediterranean.

The Middle East and the Mediterranean are still nakedly vulnerable to Russian attack. This attack might come frontally, upon Turkey, or an attempt may be made to out-flank Turkey via Iran or the Balkans. Turkey and Greece must be held at all costs. There are four major considerations in Mediterranean and Middle Eastern defensive strategy. The Southern European littoral must be held, especially Italy and Greece. The Mediterranean must be kept open for communications and supplies for SHAPE (Supreme Headquarters, Allied Powers in Europe) and whatever ultimate military coalition is formed within the projected Middle East Command. The Mediterranean is the shortest and quickest Middle East supply route and the major route for oil transport from east to west. Loss of the Mediterranean would be well-nigh disastrous. In order to hold it, North African bases must be secured. Point four is the Middle East itself. If the Middle East falls to Russia, the Mediterranean is lost and North Africa with it. Politically, geographically and geometrically, the Middle East is vital to the West; economically, it is the greatest prize in the world. Sea, air and land forces must have Middle Eastern oil to move, and civilian economies and productivity depend on *oil*.

A supreme command and a supreme commander in the Middle East is of no importance whatsoever aside from the *amour propre* of certain powers, notably Great Britain and the U. S., and chauvinistic public opinion—which will go by the boards straightway when the shooting starts. Neither SHAPE, Carney nor Gardner would object to a British commandant over a Middle East Command well coordinated with SHAPE and the Southern European Command and the U. S. Sixth Fleet.

The United States considers it absolutely essential to insure protection of the Suez Canal, either from outside aggression or from nationalist fanatics in Egypt who could endanger Allied security and supply lines in wartime. The celebrated Churchill speech in Washington in January of 1952 exposed the issue clearly, for all the world to see. The feigned embarrassment of Whitehall at this disclosure was amusing to knowledgeable observers. Egypt's outraged reaction, under the peculiar circumstances, surprised nobody.

[240]

In event of war tomorrow, or the day after, it is the considered opinion of Allied commandants in the Mediterranean and the Middle East that Russia's initial blows could be withstood, that Russia's first massive attacks could be contained, and that certain emergency measures could insure continuance of Allied Mediterranean supply. These are not the opinions of the writer, nor those of many other military experts in the Middle East.

Radar screens now offer limited protection to Allied naval and air forces in the Middle East and the Mediterranean, with the exception of the Yugoslav gap, from Jutland to Turkey's frontiers with Iran. Still imperfect, but building, this screen could offer brief warning of any all-out aerial attack from Russia aimed at destroying Allied defenses in a kind of European Pearl Harbor.

Sneak submarine attacks ultimately are more to be feared than aerial assaults, for the Russian U-boat fleet is reputedly the greatest the world has ever known—and Allied supply lines in the coming war may be even more extended than during World War II. Despite Turkish security measures, Russian submarines are believed operative today in the Mediterranean, probably from Albanian bases on the Adriatic.

The entire Atlantic Fleet soon will have its Mediterranean sea legs. There is a complete turnover in the Sixth Fleet every four months, with a replacement for every destroyer, cruiser, flattop and battlewagon, supply ship and submarine.

USAFSAC is still largely a classified matter, top secret, and Allied commandants in the Middle East and the Mediterranean are loath to discuss their liaison with the Strategic Air Command whose job it will be to drop the big bombs into the Russian interior when war comes.

The fact that the Strategic Air Command *does* envision Middle Eastern and Mediterranean operations is no secret, however. U. S. global air strategy is directed from SAC at Offutt Air Force Base at Omaha, Nebraska, and most of the vast Middle Eastern terrain is as well known to SAC's growing command of superb pilots, navigators and bombardiers as to the commander himself, four-star General Curtis E. LeMay, who is generally recognized as one of the most valuable general officers in modern U. S. history. The Eighth Air Force under SAC is located at Fort Worth, Texas; the Second at Shreveport, Louisiana, and the Fifteenth at Riverside, California, but all three are equipped to operate instantly anywhere in the world, if necessary, non-stop from their home bases. With refueling at secret advance bases and the use of advanced bomb stores, SAC's ten-engined intercontinental B-36's could carry more than 40 tons of bombs to any target in the Soviet Union.

Because SAC bases in the Middle East are less vulnerable than U. S. Air Force bases in East Anglia and elsewhere in the British Isles, Allied intelligence officers in the Middle East are well aware that Russia will undertake the most desperate means to destroy these bases—including probable suicide raids. Measures are being taken, accordingly.

In all the foregoing chapters, the author has sought to sum up the degrees of political reliability and military preparedness among potential Western Allies and probable enemies in the coming struggle with Russia in the Middle East. There will be no effort in this closing chapter to recapitulate those earlier facts and estimates for, with minor exceptions, there have been no major shifts or changes, no fundamental political realignments and no appreciable strengthening of the military sinews among the Middle Eastern, mid-Asian and North African nations involved in the mercurial events which shaped the writing of this book. Sudden political upheavals may transpire in the few short weeks before these chapters roll through the presses to publication. It is highly unlikely, however, that the swiftly gathering storm will burst without some final, igniting spark from Russia. Russia, unhappily, still has the initiative. But her time is running out.

One more Russian miscalculation could be fatal.

Such a miscalculation seems already to be in the making: *the Middle East.* Russia's Asiatic adventures have proved enormously successful, from almost every point of view. Korea, Indo-China and Malaysia, Formosa and Japan and Communist China itself have the United States, France and Britain almost hopelessly bogged down, militarily and politically, in ruinous campaigns of attrition. The drag and drain upon pinched French economy and austere Britain are almost intolerable. The sheer bloodshed, in these murderous, dirty campaigns, has so revolted Americans that they numbly accepted the peace-at-any-price formula directed from affrighted Washington. Stalin's ordnance experts—like Hitler's in Spain—used Asiatic battlefields to test new weapons, jet warplanes, tanks and radar-directed flak guns. Again, like Hitler's specialists, Stalin has discovered under battle conditions that Russian equipment is superior in many departments to Western armaments—and no time has been lost in tremendous production. While Western armaments production has crawled, in the strait jackets of machine-tool shortages, metals, top-level inertia (including the inability of the Pentagon to get blueprints off the drawing boards)—and the inclination of many American manufacturers to continue the production of electric refrigerators, automobiles and all the impedimenta of Western living, Soviet production has zoomed ahead and upward. The temptation to cite historical parallels is not only overpowering but too true to resist.

As Hitler Germany turned upon the West in 1938 with the arrogance born of overwhelming power, Western weakness, indecision and cowardice in high places, so the implacable Soviet plotters face the United States, Britain and France today in the Middle East. The parallels can and should be carried further. The American sell-out of China and Yugoslavia and the British abandonment of Poland and consistent British mishandling of Iran and Egypt, Iraq and Hashemite Jordan, and hard-headed French colonialism in Tunisia and Morocco—all come uncomfortably close to the darkling days before Danzig.

The sprawling, untidy Middle East, moreover, is aglow with the fires of revolt and the temper of its peoples and most of its leaders is one of recklessness, murder and intrigue—and a willingness to risk anything, including the holocaust of war, rather than a continuation of what is considered intolerable servitude. That the Egyptians and Iranians in particular are wrong does not alter the picture. Tunisia has caught flame and the fiery Berbers of Morocco are smoldering. Nearly fifty million peoples in one of the most dangerous areas on earth are within a touch of mass hysteria and murder.

Stalin and his lieutenants, Malenkov and Beria, have the Hitlerian blueprint. The Western world is arming, laggardly, and with agonizing paperwork and bureaucratic fuss-budgeting that has to be seen to be believed.

In a word, militarily, 1952 is Russia's year.

One year longer may be too late for Russian conquest. If

Winston Churchill retains life and office—and there seems every reason to suppose that Britain's greatest statesman will survive his severest test—Soviet aggression in the Middle East will be met by implacable Western resistance, for Britain cannot fight alone. Nor will she.

Russia's fatal miscalculation, like Hitlerian Germany's, is based upon the belief that a bankrupt, dreary and disheartened England will not again unite with unhappy and internally disunited France and a bemused but angering, incredibly powerful people in the United States to obliterate Communist Russia from the face of the earth—with the advent of aggression in an area that cannot and will not be surrendered.

Russian arrogance has at once reached its nadir and its peak. As Hitler's jack-booted *Wehrmacht* and the terrifying *Luftwaffe* once bestrode Europe, Russia's Red Army and satellite legions now menace the vulnerable West in the Middle East as Red China undertakes the diversionary engulfment of Indo-China, Malaysia and Indonesia.

It is highly unpopular to say such things. It is considered heinous to write them. The policy of sweet reasonableness, appeasement and surrender has been the watchword of Western policy vis-à-vis latter-day Napoleons since this writer has been covering wars and the journeys between them. Invariably, such policies have led only to more journeys and more wars.

It is a thing devoutly to be hoped that this forthcoming journey in 1952 might be the last one to the last war.

If it is not (and it probably is not), this writer can only add the additional hope that your sons and mine will go forth as readily to battle armed with ideas to end forever this tyranny of quasi-Napoleons—and to make a better, peaceful world at the end of it.

Vitam impendere vero was Juvenal's line, adopted by Jean-Jacques Rousseau, and it is good enough for this book. Roughly, that means to lay it on the line.

INDEX

[249]

[253]

[255]

White Oil Springs, 30
Wilson, General Sir Henry Maitland, 55, 114

Yadin, General Yagil, 68
Yalta, 144
Yassi Huyuk, 6, 7, 9
Yaver, Colonel, 32
Yemen, 5, 40, 61, 78, 183-184, 186
Young, Dr. Rodney, 7